# Glass Beads from Europe

## With Value Guide

### Sibylle Jargstorf

77 Lower Valley Road, Atglen, PA 19310

## Photo Credits

- Photographs with no reference: Author.
- Photographs with indication of collection: Made by the author with the permission of the museum or private owner.
- Photographs with *Courtesy of* indicated: Made by the indicated owner of the photo graph.
- Colored sketches: Author.
- Bead drawings: Johannes Jargstorf.
- Illustrations from books (page # and position):

      6 BL: Minutoli, 1824.
      7 B: Ibid.
      8 BR: Ibid.
      9 TR: Kisa, 1908.
      12 TL: Ibid.
      15 TR: Ibid.

17 C: Ibid.
19 T: Minutoli, 1824.
20 T: Bernatzik, 1948.
27 TR: Pazaurek, 1911.
31 TL: Kuntze, Paul H. *Das Volksbuch unserer Kolonien*. Leipzig: G. Dollheimer Verlag, 1938.
132 BC: Pazaurek, 1911.
134 BL: Schweinfurth, 1922.
134 C: Ibid.
134 TR: Mecklenburg, 1914.
135 TC: Ibid.
146 TL: Kisa, 1908.
166 BR: Ibid.
167 TL: Pazaurek, 1911.
174 TR: Kisa, 1908.

Printed in Hong Kong.
ISBN: 0-88740-839-7

**Library of Congress Cataloging-in-Publication Data**

Jargstorf, Sibylle.
    Glass beads from Europe: with value guide/ Sibylle Jargstorf.
       p.   cm.
    Includes bibliographical references and index.
    ISBN 0-88740-839-7 (pbk.)
      1. Glass beads--Europe--History.  2. Glass beads--Europe--Catalogs.  I. Title.
NK5440.B34J37  1995
748.8'5'094075--dc20         95-23106
                       CIP

Published by Schiffer Publishing, Ltd.
77 Lower Valley Road
Atglen, PA 19310
Please write for a free catalog.
This book may be purchased from the publisher
Please include $2.95 postage.
Try your bookstore first.

We are interested in hearing from authors
with book ideas on related subjects.

# CONTENTS

# FOREWORD

It is a kind of detective work to retrace the history of European glass beads. Interpretations and conclusions are required in order to connect what scarce evidence we have into an understandable picture, and every assembled picture will remain a hypothesis which has to be corrected from time to time. What makes it so difficult to retrace this history?

The beadmakers never considered their craft important enough to keep a record of it. The records regarding blown glass are neither complete nor satisfactory - yet at least we have written records from the glassmakers, while we do not even have such fragmentary records from the beadmakers. The merchants marketed and described the beads without identifiable characteristics. They used shape and weight designations, fancy names, and perhaps an indication of their color. Beads became important only to the first- or second-hand users — and they tended to spin a myth around them, ranging from the legends like those that surround the famous "aggri" beads to misleading designations like "Russian" beads.

Bead-archeology is still very incomplete and up till now the excavated beads have only supplied some of the pieces to a puzzle with many gaps.

Beads were made primarily by people hidden in deep forests or humble cottages; only in a very few cases were they made under the scrutinizing eyes of urban guilds. Yet even in the case of Muranese and Venetian bead production, the records between the 14th and 17th centuries are poorer than expected; they lack precision, and allow for different interpretations.

It has been a tiresome task - especially in the case of Muranese and Venetian beads - to separate fact from fiction. Therefore, I have tried to make it very apparent whenever I tried to combine the scarce records into a full picture.

Because of the many gaps between the direct bead-related evidence, it is vital to give the "guesswork" a good basis. Glass beads were never created "just for fun," or out of artistic fancy. Their creation required, of course, technological know-how and beadmaking skills - but those alone did not necessarily lead to large scale bead production. The start and growth of bead INDUSTRIES was less a matter of individual skills than a matter of political, economic, and social constellation, and last, but not least, the product of keen businessmen who saw the economic potential of those industries and the profit which lay in them. A good knowledge of such background facts allows us to speculate realistically. Therefore I have given much room for such background information in this work.

I have tried to give a true account of the important sources. I have even tried to re-interpret some of them, and I hope that my interpretations - whether they are right or wrong - might reopen discussions and might inspire or provoke my expert friends in Murano and Venice to research the matter deeper and to eventually contradict me.

# INTRODUCTION

Two necklaces including *rudraksha* beads made from the seeds of a tree unique to Java. A beetle "bead" from South America and cowrie-shell beads from Indonesia. Some of the earliest beads were shells, seedpods, beetles, and similar suitable elements which nature offered ready-made.

## Out of Africa

Around 130,000 years ago the first humans of distinctly modern appearance lived in Africa, and the oldest known beads have been unearthed in the region of modern Tanzania. They had been made about 50,000 years ago from ostrich shells.[1] After that, beadmaking from organic materials with striking diversity developed all over the world. Humans learned to transform almost any natural material into this ornament - yet such beadmaking remained a most tiresome task, generally involving a lot of cutting and grinding work on every single bead. A first important technological step forward in beadmaking was the use of metal and clay to produce the first types of non-organic beads. A further, and on the long run, far more important "industrial revolution" in beadmaking was the creation of vitreous beads.

[1] Jones, 1993:122

## "Ex Oriente Lux"

This book deals principally with European glass beadmaking and bead industries. But European bead art and craft has its roots in Afro-Asian glass technology and bead design and thus an important part of the book deals with this background. It does not mean to cover every aspect of ancient glassmaking but instead to indicate the important links between ancient beadmaking and the European bead industries and to give at least a faint idea of the creativity of the ancient makers. Their skill and knowledge was so great that hardly anything fundamental was left to be "invented" by the Europeans. To them was left the task to perfect and to diversify the given patterns and technologies.

Oriental bead craft was not only of central importance for European glass beads but also for glass art in general. Beadmaking guaranteed the continuity of glassmaking throughout the centuries and beadmaking gave the major impulses to create colored glass and to diversify the basic composition of glass. And yet this fundamental branch of glassmaking was much neglected. A statement of 1832 reflects the attitude which prevailed until the 20th century:

> *There is nothing peculiar in the composition of the glass made use of for this purpose (i.e. beadmaking); and although the manufacturers affect great secrecy as to the coloring substances ...it is not likely that they possess any real advantage over others in this respect, or that they have made any useful discovery different from those commonly employed in coloring glass.*[1]

[1] Lardner, 1832: 233-234

A necklace composed of small coral beads and mother-of-pearl elements from Germany, 1950s, and a necklace including two faceted Carnelian beads and one silver-mounted ivory bead, India, first half of the twentieth century. Other early beads were carved and cut from organic materials in very labor-intensive procedures.

# ANTIQUITY

## Fashions, Fakes, and Early Mass-Production of Vitreous Beads

Colorful Egyptian fashions including beaded collars (large central figure) and bugle networks (small figures).

The oldest known fayence and glass beads from the European and Middle Eastern regions (which were united by strong cultural bonds) originate from the Middle East, in an area where city civilizations had started to develop from the 5th millennium BC. They contrasted with the common farming and herding communities around them at least as much as medieval cities in Europe did with the large majority of the still-rural population on that continent. "City" in antiquity and "city" in the Middle Ages meant basically the same thing, i.e. a sophisticated hierarchical structure of the population, specialists for the various crafts and last, but not least, a quickly growing wealth - partly based on the exploitation and domination of the surrounding communities and the dependent working force within the cities and partly based upon an intricate trading network. By in 4th millennium BC, this area was already linked by a long distance trade reaching from the Mediterranean area to India and even further, and in the 3rd millennium BC it extended in the north to Scandinavia and in the south to Central Africa. The trading monopolists of this ancient "world" trade were the royals and the priests.

The urban societies enabled experts to concentrate on innovation and the masses of dependent labor force enabled "industrial" production of uncommon or luxury goods beyond their own needs. Those goods were profitably exchanged for "valuable" foreign goods. Important commodities were, in these early periods, above all metal wares; such as weapons and tools, and luxury goods; such as fine textiles and ornaments. These urban societies and their fashions led to the creation of the "industrial" bead.

## Beads and bugles

From the period between the 4th and the 2nd millennium BC, we know best small cylindrical fayence and glass beads in the colors white, (carnelian) red, (turquoise) green, and (lapis) blue. Those early non-organic beads were designed according to the patterns of quite standard beads - if not to say the simplest organic beads the period knew!

I presume that the most important stimuli for the invention of such artless, artificial beads, were the popularity of the fashions which incorporated beaded ornaments onto textiles and the custom of wearing important pectorals that did not feature one single bead, but large quantities of beads. From Egypt we know of such beaded fashions at least from the period of the Old Kingdom (2705 - 2155 BC) - and the fashions of ancient Egypt were almost as "trendsetting" as Parisian fashions several millennia later. From the 2nd millennium onwards, it is abundantly recorded how much the life style "à la façon d'Egypte" dominated the Mediterranean area. We know that the famous textile workshops of Ugarit (in modern Syria) in the 2nd millennium used to decorate their finest garments with beads made of lapis and

New Kingdom (1550 - 1070 BC) fashions including abundant beadwork around the neck and the shoulders. Such ornaments were very characteristic of Egyptian fashions.

carnelian - and similar-looking artificial beads might have offered a growing number of citizens the opportunity to dress fashionably. The spreading of such bead-consuming fashions offered the possibility of tremendous profits for those who held the "secret" of mass-producing artificial beads that looked like those which had to be carved from foreign raw materials.

Those early artificial beads had, at first glance, no direct revival in the European bead industries, yet those simple beads were in their function and basic shapes the forerunners of European "seed" beads and bugles.

## Immigrants and Innovation

The early civilizations owed their rise not only to their favored position in fecund valleys, but also to the repeated mingling of the population with dynamic immigrants. The first Mesopotamian civilization, for example, was the product of an immigration wave which presumably came originally from India. The famous Mesopotamian ruler, Sargon of Akkad (2350-2295 BC), represented an "Arabian" civilization after Bedouins from the Arabian peninsula had invaded, on repeated occasions, the "paradise" between the Euphrates and Tigris rivers. Here the rich lived in houses with up to fourteen rooms and the citizens walked on paved streets. In a similar way the rise of Egypt resulted from repeated disturbances caused by immigrants who had been attracted by the "flesh pots" of Egypt. For the early Egyptian history, various external influences were and still are being discussed, but, since European Egyptology had been started with Champollion the Younger (1790-1832), they all were marked by the (vain) attempt to prove that the resulting civilization could only be due to the influence of white people. This line of thinking (purposely) overlooks the fact that many Egyptian relics are strikingly "African" and that ancient historians, such as Herodotus, insisted upon the Negro character of the Egyptians. Egyptian arts and crafts document repeatedly this African background, and Egyptian glass bead art is but one small facet of it.

New Kingdom jewelry design: the necklace includes plenty of tiny beads which had to be laboriously cut from stones such as carnelian and turquoise.

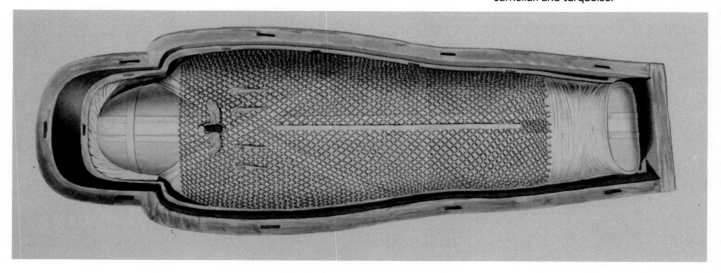

A mummy enclosed in a net of bugle beads. Such multiple bead network ornaments were exclusive to Egyptian fashions. This "design-line" had its revival in medieval Benin (modern Nigeria).

A string of modern Turkish beads with antique beads in the background, attributed to the fourth to first centuries BC. Eye beads, which are meant to protect against the evil eye, are fashionable up to the present time. Modern eye beads are primarily made in Turkey.

Various amulet pendants from Egypt, attributed to the second millenium BC. Most of the small amulets are made from fayence. Figures 2 and 25 represent two versions of ram's heads. They are the forerunners of one variety among the famous head beads in the first millenium BC. The basic design had been created in Egypt, yet knew its greatest success on the antique bead market when the Phoenicians/Carthaginians recreated it around 700 BC.

## Amulet beads - colorful bead art in fayence and glass.

We will never know exactly when glass beads were "invented," since early Mediterranean glass was generally so rich in alkalis that most early glass has disappeared forever from corrosion. Yet, we know that early workshops developed into thriving industries around the mid-second millennium, creating not only the standard beads of previous periods but also elaborate and fancy beads. Those first industries were apparently located in the north of the Euphrates-Tigris plain, in Egypt, and possibly in Northern Syria as well. The Egyptian beadmakers might have initially acquired a major part of their raw glass from the northern glass industries.[1]

The very first glassy beads had been, in the 4th/3rd millennium, fayence beads and it is generally assumed that glassmaking evolved from fayencemaking. Until glassblowing was introduced in the 1st century BC - thus making glassmaking a distinctly separate craft - ceramics, fayence, and glass were worked according to the same "cold" techniques. Egyptian fayence and glass workshops of the 15th/14th century BC operated in close connection and Egyptian glass beads of the 14th/13th century BC have as fancy (amuletic) shapes as Egyptian fayence beads. Also, the Greek beadmakers of the 14th-12th century BC created fayence and glass beads in identical design.[2]

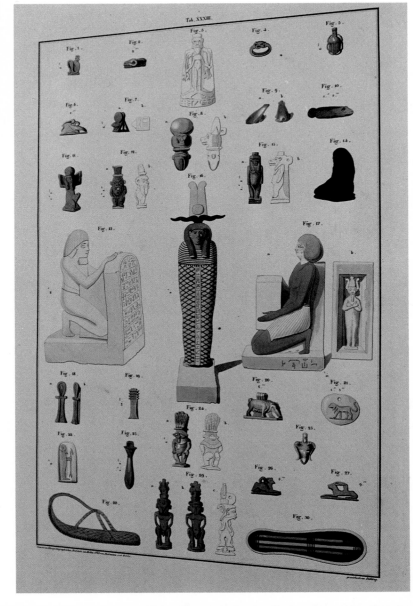

The early elaborate glassy beads from Egypt document better than any other early beads from other regions that beads did not have just a decorative value. Their magical value was far more important, and this was rendered either by their colors or their shapes. The Egyptian craftsmen excelled in creating very sophisticated naturalistic beads closely following their naturalistic bead traditions which have been traced back as far as to the reign of king Horus-Djer (2964-2912 BC).[3] Some of the finest naturalistic fayence beads which had been created in the New Kingdom period (1550-1070 BC) were those imitating various seedpods. They were strung into joyful beaded collars and were meant to conjure good harvest or to thank the gods for it. Such multi-strand beaded collars and pectorals are a typical feature of Egyptian ornament, and they represent a close link to African ornament. It has been suggested that the colorful quality of Egyptian arts and crafts might be attributable to outside influences, such as to Minoean artists who had fled to Egypt after the fall of Crete. But Egyptian art had been colorful well before that period, and there is little evidence that the preference for strong color contrasts had reached Egypt from the north; this is a most typical feature of African ornament.

The oldest elaborate and fancy glass beads are those with a magical character - the "Magical-eye" beads (see also "Eye beads"). A great variety of eye-beads made from glass had been created around the middle of the 2nd millennium BC in Egyptian workshops as well as in Mesopotamian ones.

The sudden expansion of the Egyptian glass and bead industry in the mid-second millennium had a clear political and economic background. After a long period of foreign domination, Egypt had been united again in the 16th century BC and the "golden age" of the New Kingdom period had begun. Trade - specifically with Africa - flourished and the "Egyptian way of life" was once again fashionable in the Middle East.

[1]Stern, 1994:25
[2]ibid.:157
[3]Saleh, 1986:45

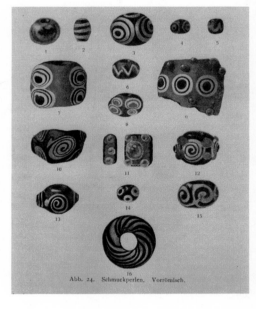

A group of antique eye beads, attributed to pre-Roman periods.

Two children wearing coral necklaces, Germany, early twentieth century. Until the present time, beads have been worn not only for their beauty but also for their magic. Since very ancient periods, corals have been worn to conjure good health and, later, red glass beads took on the same magical value.

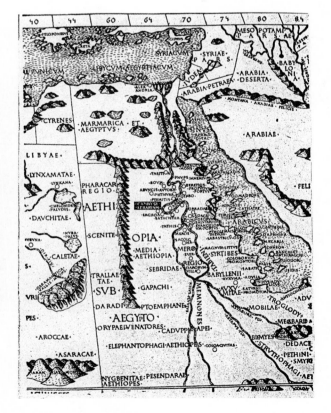

A map of ancient Egypt.

Barrel-shaped beads with pulled pattern and dotted beads from Murano/Venice, nineteenth/twentieth century. These beads represent two further splendid bead designs inherited from the Bronze Age, yet they represent the Egyptian-style design lines.

## "Classical" design vs. Egyptian exuberance in bead design

The civilizations north of Egypt, bordering the Mediterranean, and the civilizations in the Euphrates-Tigris plain, had distinctly different ornamental traditions from the Egyptians, and their bead design was clearly different. The early glass beads from Mesopotamia, which are attributable to the 16th-14th century BC, were made from almost transparent glass in generally bluish and greenish shades. The Egyptian glass beads of this period were generally made from opaque glass. And while most Egyptian glass beads had fanciful shapes, the northern glass beads had rather "classical" shapes, with cylindrical, bi-conical, globular, and barrel-shaped beads dominating. Similar to their traditional beads made from metal or semi-precious stones, the beadmakers from these areas also made flat ribbed glass elements. This design line was taken up by the Mycenean beadmakers. They created extremely elaborate cast elements which are attributed to the 14th-12th century BC.[1]

In Bronze-age Europe, a "classical" bead design, similar to the bead types popular in Mesopotamia, dominated and the amount of glass beads considerably increased from about the 13th century. The majority of the glass beads found in Europe consisted of soda-lime glass, the type of glass which predominated in Asia and the Mediterranean area as well. As the Middle East is considered to be the cradle of glass(bead)making, until very recently it had been tacitly assumed that any glass of the Bronze Age found in Europe was manufactured in the Near East or in Egypt. Yet the occurrence of such glass in Europe allows three equally valuable interpretations: 1) European glass was manufactured from the same raw materials as elsewhere, the essential ones being traded - in the same way that later Venetians got their alkalis from Syria and Egypt. 2) The Europeans imported raw glass for beadmaking. Such trading of raw glass is well recorded. 3) The Europeans imported the finished beads. The question of what happened in detail in this field is far from being resolved.

Recent analytical investigations have brought to light that some glass (beads) found in Europe have an entirely different composition - a result which supports strongly the idea of an independent European glass production as early as the late Bronze Age: a full range of glass samples (including beads and evidence for glass manufacture dating back to the 11th-9th century BC in such different European areas as Southern Ireland, Switzerland, and Northern Italy) have led to this conclusion. The glass (beads) found in those countries have important characteristics unlike the customary type of glass found in the 2nd and 1st millennia BC in the Middle East and Europe. It shows, among

Some modern Indonesian or possibly Indian beads with pulled and dotted patterns. The beads are arranged on an Indonesian food cover of the early 20th century which is abundantly decorated with bead work and mirrors; the latter are meant to deflect the evil eye.

many other compositional characteristics, high potassium oxide levels - which suggests that a new type of alkali had been used.[2] Experts are none-the-less reluctant to interpret such finds as being conclusive. Yet it is a valuable hypothesis to assume that Bronze Age Europeans knew how to manufacture glass - and made their own beads according to their own design lines - as they had indeed a very rich fayence industry and this glass shows some compositional similarities to the vitreous component of early European fayence.[3] A well rooted, genuinely European design line, in almost transparent glass beads would also explain why such patterns dominated so much Celtic glass art, and it would help to explain why this "plain" bead design persisted in Northern Europe rather than the colorful fancy glass beads which were imported from the Mediterranean. This restricted bead design dominated North European bead patterns even up to modern times - while Murano/Venice made the colorful Egyptian bead design lines available on European grounds from the late 15th/early 16th century.

The beads which have been found in Bronze Age Europe belong predominantly to three classical shapes of beads: i.e. ringlets, (flattened) spheres, and barrel-shaped beads. All three shapes occur in several sizes. The beads are made either from drawn glass tubes or by winding. The dominant colors are light-blue or blue-green - either made from soda-lime glass or from the "European" type glass. In both types of glass decorated beads appear as early as the 13th century BC with either "eyes" or spiraling decorations. The blue and green shades occur mainly in transparent glass but also occasionally in opaque glass.

The contacts between Northern Europe and the Mediterranean area were intensified again in the 12th century BC and this might well explain why we find in this period a considerably larger selection of decorated beads in Northern Europe. This supports the theory of an early independent European glass bead production following its own design lines, and meeting, in the 12th century BC, the competition of "exotic" beads from the south yet strong enough to survive itself.

Around the 8th/7th century BC the quantity of fancy decorated beads increased again, including "eye" beads with either various types of dots or spiraling decorations. The range of colors was extended. It included many more shades of blue and green and two yellowish translucent shades imitating, most likely, amber beads - as amber beads played a leading role in the European bead trade. The amount of opaque beads increased as well. Almost black beads decorated with trailings or pulled patterns have been found - beads of very "oriental" design which might have been imported but might also have been manufactured in Europe, successfully imitating "exotic" design, in the same way that today some of the finest Venetian-style beads are manufactured in Indonesia, or that Mauritanian beads take up the basic patterns of European beads yet render them even finer than they are found on the original beads.

[1] Stem, 1994:152-155
[2] Henderson, 1988:5
[3] ibid:8

Furnace-wound beads from Bavaria, 1950s (bottom) and from India, 1990s (top)—the heritage of Bronze Age bead design from Mesopotamia and Northern Europe. Similar, yet larger, disc-shaped glass pendants (as on the Indian necklace) have been found in various Mesopotamian sites. Furnace-wound beads similar to the Bavarian beads are typical of North European bead design after the late Bronze Age.

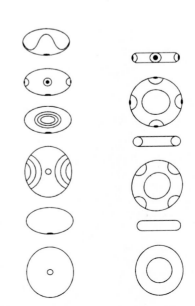

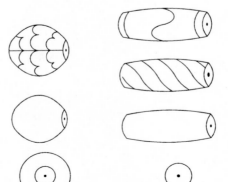

The standard shapes of glass beads found in Northern Europe during the Bronze Age. After European contacts to the Mediterranean area had been considerably intensified from the 12th century BC, a growing amount of beads with fancy decorations appeared in Europe.

Abb. 19. Groteske
Maske.
Alexandrinisch.

A head bead attributed to Alexandrian workshops, yet possibly from Carthage or the Syro-Palestinian coast, fifth to second century BC.

## Phoenician Monopoly

Around the year 2000 BC, the Oriental Empires and Egypt were no longer strong enough to impede the rise of an independent trading power in the region of modern Lebanon. This area was in a crucial position for dominating the "world" trade, as the most important west-east and north-south trade routes met here. The first trading capital which came to power was Ugarit, in the region of modern Syria. Ugarit had the leading textile industry of the period, holding the monopoly for the "world-wide" coveted purple and scarlet garments. The finest among these dresses were additionally ornamented with beads. Yet Ugarit's fame was soon eclipsed. Into the power vacuum in this area rose the Canaanites, as they named themselves, until Alexander the Great crushed their dominance. The Greeks knew them as Phoenicians.

The ancestors of the Phoenicians had infiltrated the small coastal area since the 4th millennium BC and had laid the basis for their trading empire with the timber trade to Egypt. The early Phoenicians exported luxury timber - and imported Egyptian life style. Byblos, the first Phoenician capital, had become the most important trading capital on the fringes of the Egyptian Empire by the period of the Old Kingdom (2705-2155 BC).

The final rise of the Phoenicians was also due to further favorable conditions: 1) The Mediterranean had become the cross-roads of long distance trade. 2) The last wave of immigrants from the north brought the necessary nautical skills which helped them to dominate the sea trade. 3) The economy of the old empires had been replaced by a first version of "free" production and trade which favored entrepreneurial activities. The Phoenicians realized quickly that marketing one's own products was far more profitable than shipping foreign goods, and they changed from pure traders into merchant-manufacturers. Having spread over the west, north, and south of the known world, the taste for such luxury goods as Egyptian glass (beads) and Ugarit textiles, they started their own such industries - most likely with the help of immigrant craftsmen who had left their crumbling empires to make their fortune in the capitals of flourishing Canaan. The Phoenicians succeeded so well in mass-producing those luxury goods that they were actually identified in antiquity with the "invention" of purple textiles and glass.

Two strands of translucent beads, possibly from the Syro-Palestinian coast, circa 750 BC. (Glass Museum Wertheim, Germany). These beads resemble closely the beads which have been found in Bronze Age Europe.

Sidon and Tyre were the symbols of the new Phoenician trading empire, and the prophet Ezekiel of the 6th century BC was the best chronicler of their far-reaching trading network. The upper classes of the many new feudal states found a model for their new social positions in the life style of the old empires. All around the Mediterranean, the Phoenician merchants were the bearers of Egypto-oriental fashions and way-of-life. In their important glass bead production, they took up and perfected, in the 1st millennium BC, the bead designs which basically had been created in the 2nd millennium in Egypt and Mesopotamia.

A head bead made by glass artist Cristiano Balbi, Venice, 1993; and in the background, a head bead possibly from Carthage, fifth to second century BC.

## Celtic Expansion, Cities, and Crafts

When Julius Cesar conquered Gaul he named *Oppidum* what he considered to be a small yet important Celtic settlement. This term was adopted by archaeologists to designate those highly structured Celtic settlements which represent the first city civilizations in large parts of Europe. These Celtic *oppida* were, in most cases, as large as much later important medieval cities - like Nuremberg - and they were of equal significance to Celtic crafts and industries and to their long distance trade.

The *oppida* civilization developed in the 3rd/2nd century BC after a long period of Celtic expansion. This period, since the 6th century BC, was characterized by a highly structured Celtic society with an upper class deeply interested in long distance trade to obtain rare and exotic goods to make their rank apparent. Celtic *oppida* civilization meant specialized production, mass-production for the trade, and an important intensification of the cultural and trading link to the Mediterranean area. The Celts imported such luxury goods as wine, textiles, and glass vessels and exported amber, furs, and nordic slaves.

Glass bangles from Bohemia and glass beads from Bavaria, early twentieth century. In the background are seen the Celtic forerunners of the Bohemian bangles. They were made in the important Celtic *oppidum* Manching near Munich, Germany.

Blue ringlet beads from Bavaria or Bohemia, first third twentieth century. Similar Celtic ringlet beads are visible in the background. This was a very common Celtic bead design.

A pectoral element including blue and yellow glass beads with white trailings from Southern Germany, 3rd century BC. (Landesmuseum, Karlsruhe) These beads represent a rather imaginative Celtic bead design. Most Celtic beads are monochrome. They were made from transparent glass mainly in shades of blue and yellow.

A necklace with furnace-wound beads from India, modern. Not only the colors but also the designs of Celtic beads are fashionable up to the present time. The necklace is composed of very simple elements yet it is very eye-catching when it is worn.

Celtic craftsmen excelled in many specialized crafts including metalworking - producing high quality tools, weapons, and jewelry. The jewelry and ornaments frequently included, from about the 5th century BC, mask pendants and the eye-motif so that one might suspect there to be a link between the Carthaginian head bead production and Celtic taste. Several such beads, in fact, have been found in Celtic burial sites[1], but these finds are not yet conclusive to prove such a connection.

Poseidonius, a Greek historian, traveled to Eastern Europe in the 1st century BC and referred repeatedly to the Celtic taste for eye-catching jewelry. The Celtic costume ornaments comprised important bronze parts and plenty of glass elements as well. The Celts wore lots of bangles and bracelets around their arms and legs. It is noteworthy that the Celts had, despite their close link to the Mediterranean and the early taste of their upper classes for "exotic" jewelry, their own distinctly Celtic design for glass jewelry. The standard bead types were furnace-wound ringlets and beads in the colors green, cobalt blue, violet, yellow, and black - either undecorated or ornamented with "eyes" or wavy lines. Their specialty - the glass bangles - was made from the same types of glass and generally included pinched decorations. In addition, they created very elaborate red enamelwork on metal ornaments. Celtic glassworking was restricted to these ornaments. The question whether they made their own glass or whether they imported it has not been conclusively answered. A sunken ship near Corsica reopened this question.[2] The ship, attributed to the 3rd century BC, transported cobalt blue raw glass from Rhodes, which was an important center for Hellenistic glass production.

[1]Düwel, 1985:253
[2]Dannheimer, 1993:287

## Imperial Glass Beads - From Alexander the Great to the Caesars

Alexander's far-reaching Empire, and later the Hellenistic Empire, facilitated long-distance trading of luxury goods and contributed to the flourishing glass (bead) industries in the Levante and Egypt. The consolidation of the Roman Empire in the 1st century BC, integrating Europe and Northern Africa into a huge "free-trade-zone," created an even better basis for the exchange of goods and the growth of various industries. The "Roman Community" was favorable to the production of glass beads and other such luxury trinkets, since the upper classes throughout the Roman Commonwealth had adopted Mediterranean life style and fashions. Europeans north of the Alps adopted the refined glass fashions of Egypt and Syria. Ancient Europe's glass design and production found its own independent style in the last century BC. The Rhineland became a glassmaking area which equalled, in every possible aspect, the traditional ones on the southeastern fringe of the Mediterranean.

Beadmaking in the Roman Empire was dominated by the same two contrasting design lines we know from previous periods: The colorful opaque Egyptian bead design which was now perfected in Alexandrian workshops with incredible refinement, and the transparent interpretation of "classical" design which was now produced primarily in Greek and European workshops. It seems as though glass beadmaking never became a truly Roman craft, but remained in the hands of those who had mastered it before Roman rule and continued it after the Roman Commonwealth broke apart. Among seventy terms for various Roman crafts - including five different designations for separate glass crafts - we find no word for glass beadmaking.

Abb. 31. Große Glaskugel. Sammlung von Bissing.

A huge Rosetta bead, 4 cm in diameter, attributed to antiquity. Similar overlay cane design is known from Alexandrian workshops during the Roman Empire and apparently they made similar beads around the first to third century AD as well. Yet we know meanwhile that most of the Rosetta-type beads which were attributed to antiquity even by experts up to the 20th century, are in fact the products of Muranese craftsmen.

The Muranese makers took up ancient "Oriental" patterns - yet they were apparently the first ones to create the star-like pattern within the canes not by fusing preshaped elements, but with the help of a patterned mold.

Sketch of a bead from Roman-period workshops with an exceptionally elaborate pulled pattern. The bead has an opaque blue core which is decorated with many white trailings. They were pulled in opposite directions to produce a feather-like pattern.

Three lampworked beads from Murano/Venice, first third of the 20th century. The Italian lampworkers produced a large variety of beads with pulled pattern, among them a choice of very fine, rather small oblong beads (length of the beads 1.7 cm).

Right:
Two mosaic beads possibly from Alexandrian workshops, first century BC to 2nd century AD. Each bead is carefully cut and polished at the ends, yet these flat ends are cut at an oblique angle. Apparently they had been strung into a short necklace without any spacer-beads. Presently the beads are inserted into an elaborate necklace which dates from the 1920s.

A wound bead from the period of the Roman Empire. The bead is made from opaque dark glass. The external decomposition of the glass has produced the iridescent sheen. The winding structure is visible from the slightly different shades of the iridescence.

An iridescent bead, attributed to the company WMF, Germany, mid-1920s - mid-1930s. Since the 19th century, the European beadmakers tried to reproduce the attractive sheen of the excavated (and externally decomposed) glass from antiquity. Beads got generally a luster finish with the application of ultrathin metallic layers. Only a single type of truly iridescent beads was produced in the first third of the 20th century. Those beads got their sheen from the same labor-intensive process as the famous Art Nouveau glass.

## African Trade in Antiquity

### Imperial expeditions

Egyptian trading and tributary links with Africa are recorded from the 3rd millennium BC. The early Egyptian caravans left the Nile at Elephantine (=Aswan) - an ancient name which indicates its central role in the ivory trade - and went presumably as far as Darfur (now in Western Sudan). The merchant-explorers of the 6th dynasty had already acquired the precious "raw" materials ebony, ivory, frankincense, and slaves which made the African trade so attractive to northern civilizations for the next 4500 years. The trading link with Punt - which may be placed in the area of modern Somalia - is also recorded

Three sketches of standard millefiori beads created between the 3rd century BC and the third century AD, a modern necklace with millefiori beads from Murano, and a modern Indian millefiori bead. The upper sketch shows a bead made from transparent glass with a few complex slices incorporated which are made from opaque glass. Millefiori beads were and are mostly made with an opaque glass core, yet the ancient craftsmen had already succeeded in combining transparent and opaque glass. The modern Muranese beads also have a clear core which is overlaid with two large slices.
The central sketch shows a very complex millefiori bead with star-shaped and square elements. The bead is ground flat at the ends. This method of grinding the ends was apparently quite popular in ancient times. Modern glass beads get such treatment quite frequently in Africa.
The bottom sketch of a barrel-shaped millefiori bead represents a type which dominated among the Egyptian mosaic beads since the 2nd millenium BC: a monochrome core (in ancient Egypt mostly brick-red, here black) was decorated with regular rows of flower-like slices. The biconical Indian bead has a very similar pattern.

Three men from Punt (modern Somalia) on an Egyptian relief of the epoch of Queen Hatshepsut (1490-1468 BC). The men wear necklaces with large solo beads. The wearing of solo beads was a typical African fashion and even the term "solo bead" (in Latin, *unio*) was brought by Romans from Africa to Europe in the first century AD.

from the 3rd millennium BC. Before the end of the third millennium BC, those commercial links had become systematic - but we have to wait for another 700 years until we learn which Egyptian goods were bartered for African products. The records from the period of queen Hatshepsut (1490-1468 BC) provide us with a detailed list of the "marvels of the country of Punt" which were brought to Egypt and with the information that the Egyptians carried into Punt such goods as daggers, (metal) bracelets and (glass) beads. Considering this flourishing exchange, it is not far-fetched to assume that a major part of the thriving glass bead industry of the New Kingdom period produced beads for African trade. Many of the fancy Egyptian beads of this period were not suitable for beadwork on textiles - the important luxury good for the northern markets - and they were hardly suitable for the splendid beaded collars which we know of from Egyptian paintings. So far no archeological evidence about the goods which were traded has been made available, yet we know that the Egypto-African connection expanded and that an important trading route went from the Middle Nile to Lake Chad in the 1st millennium.

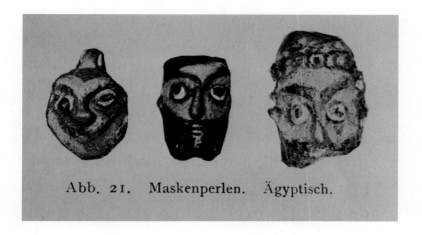

Abb. 21.  Maskenperlen.  Ägyptisch.

Three head beads attributed to Egypt yet possibly Carthage, sixth or fifth century BC. This bead design might have been created by the Carthaginians for the African market.

## Carthage trades south

Another important trading route existed long before the middle of the 1st millennium BC between North Africa and the region of the Niger river, upon which horse- or donkey-drawn carts and chariots crossed the Western and Central Sahara. The Carthaginians - from the most important Pheonician colony of Carthage - traded along this route, and thus had found their independent access to the coveted commodities from Africa, such as the elephant tusks they used to create Phoenician ivories. This famous product of Phoenician craftmanship - which cannot deny its Egyptian origins - was most successfully marketed, from the 2nd millennium throughout their entire trading empire.

Herodotus supplied us with details in the 5th century BC about further Carthaginian ventures into the African trade. They are said to have sailed along the West African coast where they traded their goods for gold. Herodotus was the last one to report that in the African trade there was "perfect honesty on both sides." We have no written record about the goods which they traded for gold and ivory, yet it is reasonable to assume that among those goods were Carthaginian/Phoenician glass beads - specifically the famous head beads which were apparently produced primarily in the Carthaginian workshops.

### Towards "the last market town of Azania" (=Africa) (Periplous of the Erythrean Sea, 1st century AD)

By the time the Phoenician trading empire was destroyed and the classical Egyptian civilization had suffered from Assyrian, Persian, Greek, and Roman dominance between the 7th and 1st century BC, we finally learn, in the 1st century AD, interesting details about export industries on Egyptian grounds which produced for the African and Indian trade. A Greek merchant-seafarer wrote a mariner's handbook for the Indian trade including a few sections on the southern extension of this business that carried ships down the East African coast as far as modern Tanzania where the merchants went mainly to acquire African ivory for export to India. The goodwill of the African kings was gained by luxury goods such as wine from Italy. Otherwise, the Africans acquired metal weapons, copper jewelry, glass beads, and textiles, in exchange for their precious goods which ranged from ivory to slaves. The glass for this African and Indian trade was not only produced in Egypt but also in the Arab trading center Mouza on the Red Sea.[1] The Arabs made their own independent trade with Africa and India. Pliny reports in the 1st century AD about the Arabian trade with Africa - the Arabs buying African spices and selling glass and metal products as well as textiles from Arabian industries.[2]

Thus the Africans might have transmitted their glass bead design impulses to the Egyptian glass bead industries as well as to the Arabian ones, and equally to the Indian bead industries - as Indian glass beads were

A map, representing the knowledge about Africa at the end of the second century AD, shows that the inner part of West Africa, the northern parts of central Africa, and the area of modern Sudan were quite well known and were integrated into the antique trading world.

African fashions in antiquity: this Egyptian painting shows various races with their typical costumes, among them one African with beaded ornaments. The "beads" are presumably cowrie shells.

Egyptian paintings and some glass fragments including one mosaic bead and one Rosetta-type bead (figure 7). Conclusive evidence for when the first Rosetta-type beads had been created is still lacking, yet we know that the basic cane design had existed before the Baroviers from Murano took up the pattern and created their famous Rosetta beads. The cylindrical mosaic bead (figure 12) corresponds with its monochrome ends to one important design line among the Egyptian mosaic beads in the period of the first century BC to the fourth century AD. The glass elements (figures 6, 9 and 10) are glass inlays of the period from the third century BC to the first century AD, and the square cane (figure 11), which is attributed to the same period, is meant to be cut into such inlays. Similar cane segments with intricate patterns were also used for making mosaic beads. In this picture, almost every person depicted is adorned with bracelets and beaded collars. This is the typical Egyptian jewelry which resembles African jewelry patterns.

part of this trade as well. Glass bead design, until modern times, was hardly ever the product of free artistic creativity but was designed according to the bead traditions and explicit wishes of the most important customers. How important the African impulses for (glass) bead design must have been already in antiquity can be deduced from the abundant bead fashions shown by the terra cotta figures of the "Nok" civilization (500 BC - 200 AD) in the area of modern Nigeria. Whoever made such abundant use of beads influenced their design as well. If we accept that African wishes influenced antique bead design, we can better understand why those "Egypto-African" design lines were reactivated later in exactly the periods when new empires and new merchants started to exploit the African trade. The colorful bead design of compound cylindrical beads and of cylindrical mosaic beads had its revival when the Roman Empire began to profit from the African trade around the 1st century AD, had the next revival around 700 AD when the "golden age" of the Afro-Arabian trade began, and a further revival when Europe started to conquer the African trade in the 15th/16th century.

[1]Stern, 1985:31
[2]Pliny, Nat. Hist. XII 42.88

A sketch of a (vessel) fragment made of terracotta from the area of modern Nigeria, Nok-culture, circa 500 BC to 200 AD. The fragment is in the collection of the National Museum Lagos, Nigeria. This figural fragment gives us an idea about West African fashions in antiquity. The person is adorned with two superimposed, multi-strand necklaces.

The white lady of Auanrhet, Algeria, attributed to 3000 BC. This rockpainting in the Tassili mountains shows traditional African ornaments and design patterns which have clear links to Egyptian ornaments. This picture represents the oldest known paintings from the area in which all paintings show great affinities to late African artwork. Some persons depicted wear, for example, masks of the same type as those still worn on the Ivory Coast. Adornments as worn by the "white lady" had been worn by Dinka men until the early twentieth century.

"Egyptian" cane design on mosaic glass fragments attributed to the ninth century AD and on modern trade beads from Murano which had been created for the African market. The oldest known cane patterns of this design are from Hellenistic Egypt of the second century BC to the first century AD, a period in which the trade with Africa was again very much intensified. It might well be possible that the antique pattern had been inspired by African design wishes.

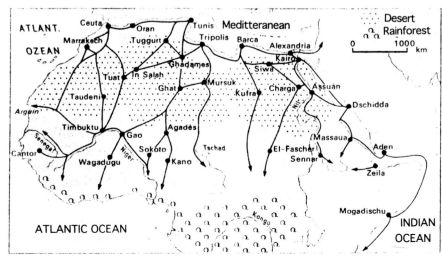

A map of the important Arabian trading routes in medieval Africa.

# MIDDLE AGES

## Buried Beads

*Bryan Faussett describes finding in many Saxon graves quantities of coloured and variegated glass beads, not so finely worked as the Roman ones, but differing greatly in shape, some made in long drops as though for earrings, some wide and flattened apparently for hanging, others were slung on knotted wire rings, and one bead had twisted gold wire...M. H. Baudot describes thirty-five tombs at Charney, Dijon; among these he discovered twenty-four complete necklaces formed of mixed amber and glass beads, the latter of every shape and colour, some like Roman mosaics, some striped, zig-zag, wavy, or spotted, spirals, circles, imitation of leaves, in fact everything that chance or the hand of the workman could conceive. It is impossible to give any idea of the variety of the beads; one necklace was formed of small glass beads, blown and moulded, into the middle of each a small piece of silver had been introduced which imitates exactly the shimmering aspect of a pearl, between each three or four pearls is placed a long blue or green bugle resembling the mummy necklaces of Egypt. These tombs are supposed to date between the fourth and fifth centuries.[1]*

A sketch of Irish "cable beads" from an Irish burial site near Dublin, ninth century AD.

The "pagan" burial habits provide us with important information about glass bead production and bead fashions. Wonderful glass beads in various designs and techniques have been found in European burial sites - but even a hundred years after Mrs. Wallace-Dunlop had collected the above information we are still in search of many answers. Innumerable beadworking sites have been excavated since that time, such as in the important trading and manufacturing settlement of Haithabu in North Germany which flourished in the 9th-11th century. However, in most cases we don't know where the glass for making the beads might have come from as trading of raw glass had become quite customary. Our knowledge about beadmaking in this period is scarce for several practical reasons, such as the shortage of written sources, but it has also been limited because of well rooted preconceptions about the "dark ages" of European glassmaking. The general tendency was, until recently, to attribute the "better" beads which had been found in Northern Europe almost automatically to a Mediterranean origin. It will take some time to expunge wrong ideas about Medieval glassmaking in Europe, but we know from recent research and glass analyses that European glassmaking in post-Roman times was far more creative and diversified than we had previously been willing to concede.

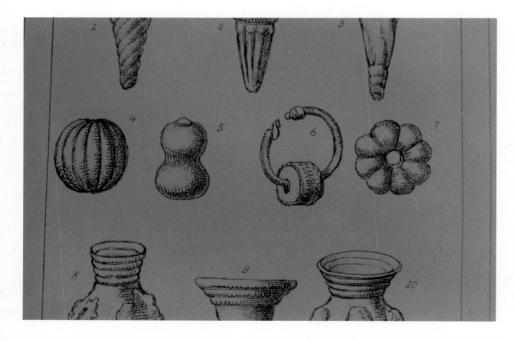

Standard shapes of beads as they were found, and possibly made, in early medieval Europe.

Sketches of four beads from the 9th/10th centuries, excavated in Northern Europe. Their origin has not yet been fully ascertained yet they were most likely made on ex-Roman territory in northwestern Europe. These beads continue the traditions of Egyptian mosaic bead patterns. This bead design had been further refined during the Roman Empire and it knew its highest perfection in early medieval periods. These complex beads are generally quite large. Beads of the upper type are up to four centimeters in diameter. Most frequently used elements on these beads are swirls and checker boards. The elements are quite simple but the beads excel by their high complexity. Their colors are much more subdued than on Egyptian or "Roman" mosaic beads. A greyish blue and a greenish yellow dominate, accentuated with small amounts of brick red.

Beads from a Pomeranian burial site, seventh century AD. These glass beads originated in the Rhinelands. Recent research has revealed that Thuringian merchants were largely involved in a long distance trade, including glass and glass beads, from the Rhinelands through Thuringia and Poland to Byzantium.

From the trading center of York in the north, to the central region with glassmaking in the dense forests such as the Spessart or the Argonne Forest, and down to the Provence which was of crucial importance to the Medieval "world" trade, we know of important glassmaking centers where between 500 and 1000 AD glass was made according to various technologies and in sophisticated designs. The general assumption that the inner-European glass trade slackened in post-Roman periods has also been proven to be false. Meanwhile, we know a lot more about Medieval blown glass from Northern Europe, but our knowledge about the beads from this area is still rudimentary - with a few better researched areas such as England and Ireland.

From the early Christian era in Ireland (6th - 10th century), we know of various ecclesiastical sites where glassmaking as well as glassworking took place, including the manufacture of glass beads. In Dunmisk, Ireland, for example, beads of the 6th-8th century have been found, in which "Mediterranean" glass technology (i.e. soda-lime glass) was combined with typically Celtic technology (such as the use of lead-tin-oxide to achieve opaque yellow glass). [2] The bead fragments found prove the making of extremely sophisticated beads such as the Irish "cable" beads and millefiori beads of definite European origin. While the other glass items made in the monasteries were clearly meant for ecclesiastical use, the beads were presumably meant as gifts. We know that Christian missionaries of that period gained the goodwill of the people and rulers by tempting them with "exotic" gifts, just as a few centuries later the Africans were won for European interests.

From further glass (bead) finds in England, Germany, Poland, and the Czech Republic - attributable to the period 800-1000 AD - we have learned that not only blown glass, but beads as well, were made from various types of genuinely European glass. The different basic types of glass indicate not only a flourishing glass industry but also the variations within each type - such as many types of potash-lime-glass - indicate active production and experimentation by the European glassmakers.

The Europeans knew how to make fine glass and fine glass beads - but as European fashions didn't yet favor an important use of beads, and as there weren't yet important customers for glass beads, there was no need to further extend this highly developed craft into real industries.

[1] Wallace-Dunlop, 19th century:207/208
[2] Henderson, 1991:248/249

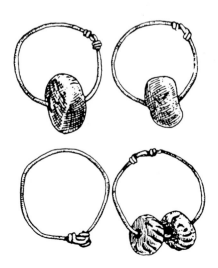

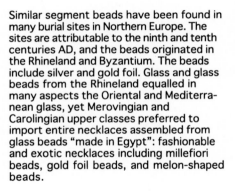

Similar segment beads have been found in many burial sites in Northern Europe. The sites are attributable to the ninth and tenth centuries AD, and the beads originated in the Rhineland and Byzantium. The beads include silver and gold foil. Glass and glass beads from the Rhineland equalled in many aspects the Oriental and Mediterranean glass, yet Merovingian and Carolingian upper classes preferred to import entire necklaces assembled from glass beads "made in Egypt": fashionable and exotic necklaces including millefiori beads, gold foil beads, and melon-shaped beads.

Coiled green "segment" beads, small blue beads and one large lampworked bead from Turkey, modern. Old beadmaking traditions survive in the Turkish bead industries. Segmenting and coiling allows for higher productivity. The thus pre-divided cylinders are frequently broken into small beads.

## Vikings and Vitreous Crafts

The Vikings, in a similar way as the ancient Phoenicians, were versatile traders and colonists. During the Viking era, continental Europe was still in search of a stable structure, while the three kingdoms in the north were strong enough to be dominant trading partners for the continental countries and competent trading partners for the eastern Empires such as Byzantium or Persia. Since the 8th century, their trading empire comprised a series of international trading and manufacturing centers such as Dublin (Ireland), York (England), Ribe (Denmark), Haithabu (Germany), Birka (Sweden), and Lagoda (Russia). Adam of Breme - a well known chronicler of the period - wrote in 1075 about Wollin, one of the trading centers on the Baltic, "it is one among the most important cities in Europe, housing a multitude of European (nationalities) as well as Greeks and other foreigners. The town is filled with the commodities of the northern people (=Vikings)." In each of those trading and manufacturing centers, glass was worked and fine glass beads were made - yet it appears that still no real bead industry was established. At least

A necklace with thirty-six beads from a Finnish burial site of the eleventh century AD (Courtesy of National Museum of Finland, Helsinki. Photograph: R. Bäckman, 1992). The necklace was part of a costume ornament which included additionally important bronze elements which had been crafted in Scandinavia. The glass beads and the Arabian coins had been imported from Central Europe and from the Middle East.

A sketch of dresses and ornaments in early medieval Europe. These European ornaments included necklaces and dangling strands, hanging down from bronze fibulas - yet the necklaces and strands were crafted from metal.

one external and one internal reason accounted for this. First, there was no economic need for the Vikings to enter this business on a large scale. They had no direct trading partners requiring large amounts of beads, and their traditional export goods - furs, slaves, leather, pergament, amber, and weapons - were sufficiently desired on the southern markets so that there was no need to establish new industries. Secondly, the Scandinavians tradition-ally excelled in a series of ornamental crafts based on metalworking. Their fashions comprised abundant ornaments of this type, yet beads played a minor role in them.

The amount of beads found in Viking burial sites has been generally not higher than fifty beads per grave - while a single tomb in Africa of about the same period comprised 10,000 beads.[1] The very restricted use of glass beads in Scandinavian costumes even allows for the assumption that most of the beads which were found in the burial sites had arrived in the north not as trading goods but as presents or souvenirs, by marriage or through robbery.

[1]Eyo, 1983:18

Sketches of beaded ornaments which were excavated in Lithuania. The burial site dates from the 11th century. These ornaments are uncommonly rich in glass beads (blue and yellow) but even here dominate the bronze elements.

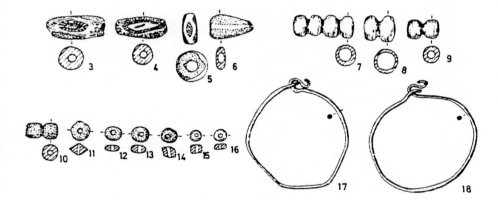

Several beads from a burial site in Thuringia of the eleventh century AD. The find includes blue, yellow, and green beads and two millefiori beads as well.

## Ecclesiastical Needs and Colored Glass

The necessary knowledge and skills required for making glass and glass beads existed in early Medieval Europe above all in the monasteries. The occidental monkery - dedicating life to praying and working, i.e. *ora et labora* - had been initiated by Benedict of Nursia (circa 480 - 547). The famous *Handbook About Various Crafts (Schedula diversarum artium)*, which had been written by the Benedictine "Theophilus," documents the active search of this order to compile the knowledge in crafts of their period and to apply this knowledge to the manufacture of their splendid ecclesiastical utensils and ornaments in their monasteries. Theophilus, alias Roger of Helmarshausen (a Benedictine monastery upon the river Weser in Germany), was a trained goldsmith yet knew about vitreous crafts of his period ranging from Russian enameling in the east to French windowmaking in the west. He also dealt with certain questions on glassmaking in his manual. We learn from this text that European glassmaking of the 12th century relied upon two sources - the traditional one still being Byzantium, and the other located in Western Europe somewhere between the Argonne Forest (Belgium) and the Spessart Forest (Germany).

The main task for medieval glassmakers in Northern Europe was the making of colored windows. The early beginnings of this art have survived in the monastery church of Tours (France), which, in the 6th century, already had

A German woodcut of the fourteenth century depicting the legend about Saint Dominic receiving the original rosary.

A *paternoster* maker (rosary bead maker) shown cutting the beads from organic materials from Germany, fifteenth century. Glass was only among the many materials which were used for making rosary beads. Only in the eighteenth century did glass rosaries become the dominant type.

King David as shown in a glass window of the dome in Augsburg, Germany, eleventh century. The production of colored glass for windows was taken up in Northern Europe around the sixth century AD. The skills acquired in composing various types of colored glass for the windows provided an ideal basis for making glass beads.

A German woodcut of the sixteenth century depicting a nun of the Saint Brigid order who wears a rosary with all beads of identical size. Early rosaries did not have the standardized sequence of beads as is found on modern rosaries.

A German woodcut of the sixteenth century depicting a nun with her rosary. This rosary has small and larger beads and a pendant, yet it is still not the same as modern rosaries.

windows inlaid with colored glass - a design which had been inspired by Arabian window art. Italy, however, adopted mosaic art from Byzantium as the main ornament for its churches. The need for colored window glass grew so high that it was soon produced in independent workshops. Otherwise the Benedictine monasteries remained the center of vitreous craftmanship: the craftsmen of the Benedictine monastery Corvey (Germany) made not only colored glass for windows between the 9th and 11th century, they also made blown glass. This production line was most likely initiated by Charles the Great, who had built a splendid palatinate in nearby Paderborn during 776/78. The making of artificial gems is equally recorded from the Benedictine monasteries since the 7th/8th century as well in England as in Germany.[1] The origin of early beadmaking within the boundaries of Benedictine monasteries has not yet been researched, but there is no reason to believe they shouldn't have started beadmaking as soon as the "fashion" of decorating ecclesiastical garments and utensils with beadwork began. In Venice, it is recorded that the making of glass beads was originated in the 14th century by the makers of artificial gems. Because the step from making gems to making beads is so small, and would depend solely on the respective demand, we can presume bead manufacture in some Benedictine monasteries from at least the 13th century. The oldest known pieces from church treasuries that include small beads date from the second half of the 13th century.

Shortly afterwards, the Catholic church created another important demand for (glass) beads with its official introduction of the "paternoster" string for use of the Christian population. The invention of this praying tool was met with enthusiasm, as for most people it was the only ornament they were permitted, and it created an enormous demand for beads which could not be satisfied solely with beads worked one by one using the time-consuming techniques. In the beginning, this might again have been a task for the Benedictine craftsmen skilled in gemmaking - specifically as the earliest vitreous prayer "beads" were possibly even glass stones mounted into metal frames and combined into prayer crowns - similar to the silver-mounted rock-crystal strings from the 11th/12th century.

A host (Holy Communion wafer) holder from Lower Saxony, Germany, from the second half of the thirteenth century. The beadwork is composed with glass beads and tiny pearls. Such ecclesiastical utensils were apparently the first items which were decorated with beadwork including tiny glass beads.

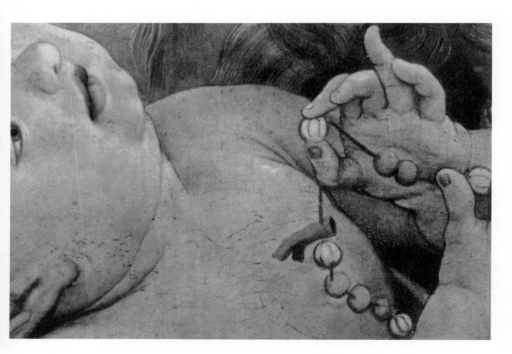

A seventeenth century painting showing the Holy Child holding a rosary which includes a coral branch and other amulets. The early rosaries were, in fact, amulet strings and their function as a counting tool was of secondary importance.

With these two ornamental initiatives, the church and the monasteries promoted the European glass bead industries in a decisive way. This specific demand for prayer beads influenced bead-related terminology: until this time, Northern Europe knew the general term "Krallen" for beads - a designation derived from one frequently used material for beads, i.e. coral. Added to this now were various terms derived from the use of prayer beads. For example, in Southern Germany, the terms "Paterla" - from "Paternoster" - and "Betl" - from "beten" (=to pray) came into being. Similarly, the English term "bead" derives from the Old English word "biddan" which means "to pray." In Murano and Venice, the first and only designation for glass beads after the 14th century was "paternostri."

[1]Webster/Backhouse, 1991: 218

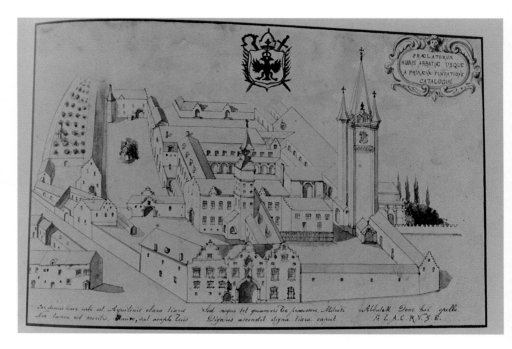

A Russian icon abundantly decorated with beadwork dating from the eighteenth or nineteenth century. The use of glass beads for ecclesiastical beadwork continued to be of great importance and even caused entirely new beads to be created. The famous gold bead of Giacomuzzi (see chapter 4) was explicitly conceived for such purposes.

A Benedictine Abbey around 1700. The Benedictine monasteries were centers of knowledge and splendour. Abbot Hugo from the Benedictine Abbey of Farfa (fifty kilometers from Rome) said, in the ninth century, "...in the whole kingdom of Italy none compared to this monastery in its splendour..." The monasteries of the Benedictine order were also centers of industry of all kinds, and of them, many produced both literary and archeological evidence for making glass.

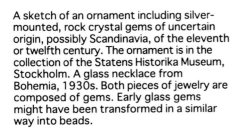

A sketch of an ornament including silver-mounted, rock crystal gems of uncertain origin, possibly Scandinavia, of the eleventh or twelfth century. The ornament is in the collection of the Statens Historika Museum, Stockholm. A glass necklace from Bohemia, 1930s. Both pieces of jewelry are composed of gems. Early glass gems might have been transformed in a similar way into beads.

## Cities and Crafts

Many of the settlements of craftsmen and merchants around the medieval monasteries and castles developed into market towns during the 11th century. Three hundred such market places existed around 1000 AD between the rivers Rhine and Elbe. Around 1300, their number had risen to about 3000, and a third among them had gained city privileges, which meant personal freedom for the citizens and an independent administration. Originally, this administration was in the hands of a few important patricians, but in North European cities the craftsmen and merchants fought successfully for their civil rights, and since the 13th century had participated fully in the government of their cities.

View of Nuremberg - a center of bustling trade. Nuremberg was world-famous for its skilled craftsmen in glass and metal since the Middle Ages.

The constant rise of these free cities was guaranteed through economic privileges, such as the "staple right," which obliged passing merchants to offer their commodities in the city. Another important privilege was the "ban mile," which prohibited craftsmen and merchants from settling within a certain area around the city, thus preventing competition from industries which could not be fully controlled by city guilds.

The cities became rich because of the heavy taxation upon trade, and strong because they united. The strongest among these city communities in the 12th - 14th centuries were the Hanse cities, which monopolized the seatrade in the North Sea and the Baltic, and the landtrade north of the Alps. Among many other goods, they traded an important amount of glass crafted in the dense forests of Northern Europe. Due to the lack of written sources, our knowledge about this medieval "Forest" glass fell victim to deeply rooted preconceptions, such as:

- Medieval glassmakers north of the Alps were not able to produce crystal clear glass,

- Any crystal glass which had been found in Northern Europe was imported from either the Middle East, the Mediterranean, or Venice,

- The northern glassmakers produced exclusively potash-lime-glass,

- Any European glass with elaborate design came from Venice.

Recent research has totally overthrown this picture, although it is still a puzzle with many gaps. However, conclusive evidence states the following regarding glass production since at least the 12th/13th century:

- Crystal-clear glass was produced at least in Southern France but most likely also in other regions such as west of the Rhineland.

- The glassmakers north of the Alps produced soda-lime-glass, potash-lime-glass, and lead-glass.

- Up to the 13th century in Northern Europe, lead glass was worked mainly into small items such as beads, ringlets, and gemstones, and since the 13th century was worked into colorful blown glass.

- The technological diversity of this European glass was matched with an equally great variety of design, some of which were extremely sophisticated.

Medieval glass from Northern Europe also had a "worldwide" great reputation. There are many records to document this, such as the famous contract of 1215, in which a certain Arnulfus of Basle promised to deliver the finest mirrorglass to Genoa, from whence it was most likely traded either to Spain or to the royal courts of the West African kingdoms.[1]

North European glass production slackened down for a short while in the 14th/15th century due to dramatic shortages in raw material. Many landlords in Western Europe made drastic cuts in their timber provisions for the glassworks, and Venice had used its strategic position to impede the import of raw materials from the Middle East.

The history of medieval glass in Northern Europe is still being rewritten, but we already know that the glassmakers had such a deep knowledge in making fine glass that they were well prepared to enter the bead business - as soon as it promised to be a profitable one! The church and the monasteries had created a need for glass beads and caused an active response among glassmakers since the early 14th century. The immediate response of the North European glassmakers is proven through the records of an established glass bead trade by the 14th century (see page 31). Beads..")

[1]Krüger, 1991:319

⊙ Captial

• Important Trading Place

Encircled Areas:

Three dominant trading areas

a)Netherlands:
    Antwerp, Bruges, Brussells, Gent
b)Southern Germany:
    Augsburg, Nuremberg, Regensburg

    Genoa, Pisa, Venice

——— Routes
---- Waterways

A map showing the important trading centers and routes in medieval Europe around 1400.

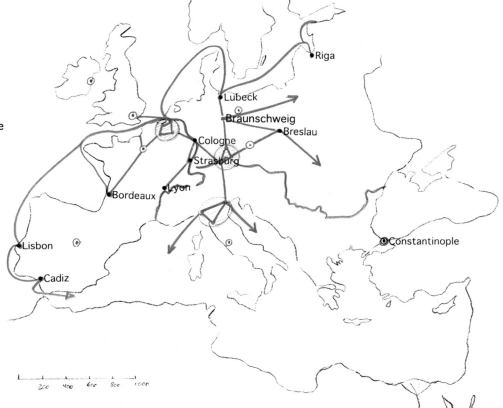

A book illustration which includes a map of the Hanse cities, a depiction of a Hanse *Kogge* (the typical trading ship of the Hanse merchants) and, at the top, the Hanse representation in London.

A small region in the glassmaking area of the Bavarian Forest. At the request of the Duke Albrecht the Fifth, the geographer Philipp Appian drew a complete map of Bavaria in the period 1554 to 1561. He included with it a detailed description of the area and indicated for the Bavarian Forest, "...here are found many glass works (producing) blown glass, exceptional mirror glass and glass beads..." He indicated on his map ten glassworks in the Bavarian Forest.

## Bavarian beads to Breslau and Nuremberg

After 1300, important medieval glass bead industries were soon started within the reach of the old trading capital Regensburg, and the new trading capital Nuremberg. Regensburg had started its career as Castra Regina, a Roman stronghold on the eastern border of the Roman Empire. Because Regensburg is situated on the Danube, it has never lost its importance as a thriving staple in the trade between Northern Europe, the Byzantine Empire and later the Ottoman Empire. Since 739, Regensburg was also a very important Catholic stronghold. The First (1096-1099) and the Second (1147-1149) Crusades passed through Regensburg, and the Third (1189-1192) was actually started there. Nuremberg, on the other hand, became a new center of motion in European trade in the 13th century. The routes that linked the Hanse cities to the North Italian trading centers and which connected Paris and the Dutch trading capitals to Constantinople and the Levante both met in Nuremberg. Such an important trading position was favorable to the growth of crafts and industries, and paternoster maker guilds are recorded in Nuremberg since the 13th century. These early urban crafts-men began making the beads from organic materials, but this production line was apparently soon followed by glass beadmaking. The glass beads came from the Bavarian/Bohemian Forest, while in Nuremberg itself, glass beadmakers presumably only existed during the 16th century and part of the 17th century. A "Perleinmacher" (=beadmakers) regulation of 1535 required the making of yellow and green beads for becoming a bead master in Nuremberg.[1] Glass production in the Bavarian Forest dates back to Celtic periods, while the medieval beginnings of glassmaking in this area are closely linked to the activities of two Benedictine abbeys; Niederaltaich and

Ecclesiastical beadwork from Lower Saxony, first half of the fourteenth century, composed of pearls, coral beads, and green and black glass beads.

A glass mirror with tiny glass beads from Germany, thirteenth century (Heimatmuseum Zorge). The use of glass beads in ecclesiatical beadwork was apparently soon followed by a restricted use in profane ornaments. It is not known where the small beads on this mirror had been made, but they are definitely not of Venetian origin.

Rott on Inn. These abbeys wanted to improve the economical infrastructure of their fiefs, yet the dense forests and the rough mountains were not appropriate for rural exploitation. Glassmakers were considered the only profitable settlers. The abbey Niederaltaich started the settling of glassmakers on their grounds around 1300.[2] The glassworks Frauenau and Rabenstein lit their furnaces before the mid-14th century.[3] Rabenstein was created exclusively for beadmaking.[4]

We can learn from merchant records covering 1383-1407 that glass beads were sold on a continuous basis from Regensburg to Nuremberg and to Breslau (Wrozlaw/Poland), where they were strung into rosaries.[5] This bead trade was based on the bead industry of the Bavarian Forest, which Regensburg was situated directly on the border of. The two different destinations for the beads reached two international trading routes; Breslau was an important center of commerce on the main road to the Black Sea and to Persia, and Nuremberg was on the main route to the Levante, passing through Venice.

The Rabenstein glassworks, which later produced fine blown glass, had already been started as a "Paternosterhütte"; a beadmaking glassworks. This practice was continued in the Bavarian and the adjoining Bohemian Forests during at least the next two centuries, and most likely spread to the Gansauer glassworks near Winterberg (Vimperk/Czech Republic), to name one of the early glassworks on the Bohemian side, which had existed since at least 1359.[6]

[1] Pazaurek, 1911:6/7
[2] Verhandlungen, 1856:209
[3] Sellner, 1988:5
[4] Poschinger, 1921:54
[5] Verhandlungen, 1890: 150
[6] Blau, 1941:89

## Beads and business

The unique abundance of written sources from Murano and Venice and the uncontestable richness of Muranese and Venetian bead production since around the second half of the 16th century, had contributed to the creation of many legends about the beginnings of this bead production, but the start of beadmaking in the "Serenissima" was apparently much more restricted than we would wish to believe.

### *Between Orient and Occident*

After the Roman Empire had split, Venice became the bone of contention between two important empires. The Venetians knew how to make the best of this difficult situation; by gradually strengthening their independence, and securing important trading privileges for themselves. For example, their military assistance to Alexios the First in 1082 gave them tax free trade throughout the entire Byzantine Empire. Today, we can hardly imagine what this privilege meant for the expansion of the Venetian economy in a period when merchants were usually harassed daily on their long distance trade by innumerable rulers and cities wanting to have their share of the trading profits. In a treaty with Henry the Fourth in 1095, the Venetians extended their existing privileges in such a way that the merchants of the "Holy Roman Empire" were no longer allowed to trade beyond Venice without first offering their commodities in the city. This basic trading right ensured that the Venetians would know from now on exactly which goods were "en vogue" on the international market, and a majority of the European merchants were thus cut off from their direct and stimulating contact with the Orient.

Artificial gems of the nineteenth century. The gem makers ( *veriselli* ) were the first recorded makers of glass beads in fourteenth century Venice.

### *The pioneers of Venetian glass art*

The research of the Italian glass expert Gasparetto has revealed that even the Venetian glass industry has its roots in Benedictine glassmaking. Yet the early glassmaking in some of the Benedictine monastaries in the regions of Venice alone couldn't have caused the exceptional rise of the Venetian glass industry in the following centuries. Up until the 13th century, Venice as a glassmaking center was of no greater importance than quite a few others in Europe, but the city ranked first as a trading capital, thus becoming a focal point of attraction for craftsmen wanting to make their fortune. Italian and Greek glassmakers in particular were attracted by the Venetian wealth and bustling trade since around the 11th century. We know little about the Venetian

The important *Fondaco dei Tedeschi* trading and storing center in Venice was founded because Venice held the "staple right" for North European commodities which were traded to the important Oriental markets. Thus, the local Venetian authorities were able to control, with scrupulous care, trade between the Northern and Eastern empires.

Sketches of important leadglass vessels/ vessel fragments from Northwest Europe, 13th/14th century. These glasses/tazze are the forerunners to the splendid stemmed glasses from 16th century Venice. The brilliant emerald green glass was found in Braunschweig. It is presently in the collection of the Landesmuseum Braunschweig. It was most likely made before 1278. The bowl rests upon a stem which is surrounded by five scroll brackets. The bowl is decorated with four raspberry prunts. The amber-colored stem fragment was found in London. Similar items made from leadglass were found almost exclusively in Northwest Europe and mostly in Hanse cities. Such glasses document the high rank of the medieval glassmakers in Northern Europe. They should not have had any difficulty entering the field of beadmaking as soon as the necessary demand was there.

glassmakers of the 11th and 12th century, but at least two of the three early names which we do know apparently came from Greece. The records of the 13th/14th century confirm an important immigration of Italian glassmakers mainly from Padua - a town whose economy possibly suffered from a Venetian "ban mile" - and of glassmakers from Greece and Dalmatia. The 14th century brought an important and affluent group of Florentine glassmakers. These early foreigners did not come to Venice to spy on Venetian glassmaking secrets, but enriched the city with variformed glassmaking skills brought from the places where they originated from, and contributed decisively to the Venetian "miracle" of glassmaking. While Byzantine glassmakers lost their economic basis in a crumbling empire, and other European glassmakers began to suffer heavily from impediments imposed upon them by their landlords who found more profitable use for their forests, the "Serenissima" favored the establishment of an export-oriented glassmaking industry with vast economic potential.

### Venetian beads

The mythical origin of the Venetian glass bead story began in the 13th century with Marco Polo as its inspiration. The real beginning, however, occurred in the 14th century and has been located there by Luigi Zecchin, the most competent expert in the matter of Muranese/Venetian glass: The Venetian makers of artificial gems offered locally made glass beads for the first time in the 1340s.[1] The first gemmaker who became a beadmaker appears in 1371 in the Venetian records.[2]

Some indications in the Venetian sources - which can be differently interpreted - combined with our knowledge of the splendid achievements in later periods made us imagine the continuous growth of a beadmaking industry in the decades which followed the introduction of this "novità." This picture is not backed by any conclusive record. Further gemmakers might have followed the example of this "William the Beadmaker" - but the local records, which deal in scrupulous detail with every important event in the glassmaking scene, tell little to nothing reliable about glass BEADmaking, yet much about glass GEMmaking. And the Muranese makers were apparently not yet involved in beadmaking at all!

We don't learn from the Venetian records what those early beads looked like, but a record from Assisi written in 1395 tells us that the Venetians produced yellow beads.[3] They may have done this to imitate the much coveted amber beads - specifically as those "veriselli" - the gemmakers - were so well trained in imitating natural materials. As regards the size and the shape of the beads we can deduce from the standard size of rosary beads and from the gemmaking background of the makers that those beads were at least pea-sized and either faceted or round. Just as gemmakers cast their gems in molds, early beads might have been molded in the same way. Possibly, the early makers adopted a winding technique as well. It would make sense to assume there was an early winding of the beads around a spit, because the adoption of such a technique might explain why local beadmakers later began to transform large cane segments from Murano into beads by reheating them upon a spit (see also pp. 52-53).

After "William the Beadmaker" had appeared, the Venetian records remain more or less silent for nearly 100 years regarding glass beadmaking. The commercial and political background might explain why Venice was not a forerunner in this craft. Venetian imperialism and trading politics had been oriented towards Byzantium and further east, as these areas appeared to be the most lucrative in the known world. The travels of Marco Polo in the 13th century clearly demonstrate which markets the Republic was aiming at. This part of the world created an important demand for the production of artificial gems, a fact deeply reflected in the Venetian glass industry, but no major motivation for making glass beads.

While the Venetians had acquired the quasi-monopoly for trade in the Byzantine Empire since the 11th century, its Italian competitors and enemies, the Republics of Genoa and Pisa, had acquired important trading privileges on the North African coast. In 1236, Genoa had also been successful in its fight for tax exemption further east on the African coast, including Tripoli, the starting point of the trans-Sahara trade.

Thus Venice missed out on possible early motivation for glass beadmaking, which might have reached Europe from North Africa between 1200 and 1400. Venice was not as exposed to the inspirations for making glass rosary beads as were Augsburg and Nuremberg, for example. Venice was lying on the fringes of the troubled Catholic world, and the seven Crusades, which certainly induced the making of rosary beads, passed far away from Venice except for a single one, while the three most important Crusades went right through Augsburg and Nuremberg.

[1]Zecchin III, 1990:15
[2]Zecchin I, 1987:26
[3]ibid.:31

Genoa in the fifteenth century. The trading and seafaring capitals of Genoa and Pisa competed with Venice in the Mediterranean area.

## Golden Age of Afro-Arabian Trade

The charisma and of power of Mahomet's successors had been making the old structures around the Mediterranean crumble since the 6th century AD. The Arabian Empire, which started to grow in the 7th century, stretched from Spain to India in its best periods and comprised a major part of Africa. The Indian Ocean trade knew a second peak period in this era. The Africans exported their customary luxury goods, and China and India traded the same commodities that were desired in Europe into the East African kingdoms, from where the Inner African trade brought at least some into the West African empires. Yet the selection of goods for Africa comprised one more product which was apparently of little to no interest for the Europeans - the glass beads.

## The Kingdoms Beyond the Sahara

Our knowledge about the medieval empires in West Africa is still fragmentary, but excavations in modern Nigeria confirm the importance of beads in the fashions of at least some African kingdoms and how much this beadwork resembled ancient Egyptian beadwork, thus supporting, along with other facts, the idea of a strong cultural link between ancient Egypt and the African West.

Close to 60,000 glass beads had been found on a single site dating back to the 9th/10th century AD.[1] Such an important demand for glass beads had necessary consequences for the supplier/producer: he was most likely inclined to create beads according to the explicit wishes of such an important client, and the demand for such quantities of glass beads inspired technological progress. It is no wonder then that we find, among beads in Nigeria, sophisticated compound drawn beads reminiscent of 19th century beads. The original provenance of those beads is not yet fully ascertained. Islamic glass, made from or including cane segments, attributed to about the same period indicates that at least some of the better beads might have come from the traditional glass and beadmaking areas in the Middle East - arriving in Africa most likely via the East-Coast trade. Many reports about the trans-Sahara trade indicate that glass beads arrived in the West African kingdoms from the east coast rather than from the north or Egyptian merchants from the northeast.

The Western Sudan trade was clearly dominated by the bartering of gold for European luxury goods (in our modern sense of the word) and for salt, which was as much a luxury good in medieval Africa as in medieval Europe:

A bronze head of a member of the royal family from the Kingdom of Benin, Nigeria, 16th century. (Museum für Völkerkunde, Leipzig) Such heavily beaded ornaments were the typical royal insignia. These are composed of large bugle beads of a size used nowhere but in Africa in this enormous quantity. Around 1500, German and Muranese beadmakers sent beads of this shape to the Levantine trading centers from where the beads were presumably traded to Africa. In the nineteenth and twentieth centuries, the export of Muranese beads to Africa was once again based largely upon beads of this shape.

*It is a wonder to see what plenty of merchandize is daily brought hither...horses bought in Europe for ten ducates are here sold againe for forty ducates...the scarlet of Venice or of Turkie cloth is here worth thirty ducates...but of all other commodities salt is the most extremely deere...and hither are brought divers written bookes out of Barbarie (=western part of the North African coast) which are sold for more money than any other merchandize.*[2]

The oldest record which we have regarding medieval glass bead trade in West Africa comes from Al Bekri, an Arab from Granada, Spain, who collected what the Muslim west knew about the lands beyond the Sahara in the 11th century. He gives us tantalizingly brief information, noting that gold was bartered in Ghana for salt and glass beads. His reports about this kingdom, which had its roots in the 6th century AD and which flourished between 800 and 1240, are far more detailed in many other aspects. We learn from him that royal exploitation by taxing trade and production was almost identical to European habits and that court life surpassed in splendor by far any European court.

[1]Eyo, 1983:19
[2]Africanus, 1896:830

## "Meadows of gold and mines of gems" (Al Mas'udi, 10th century)

The first city-states of Southern Africa were founded around the 10th century AD in the Limpopo basin. They had close trading links with the East African coast and it has been suggested that they rose to prominence because it was the first area in the interior of South Africa to be integrated into the Indian Ocean trading network. In the center of a thriving economy stood African ivory - exchanged for, among other (luxury) goods, Persian ceramics and Indian glass beads. The oldest beads that have been excavated are pale blue-green and yellow cane segments. In some cases these beads were heated and reworked into large locally made beads. Another later variety had the ends smoothed down by reheating. This variety was successfully traded from India to Africa until the 19th century.

The early Arab traders were not yet based on the East African coast but visited a number of "collecting places" along the coast - while the trade between those itinerant merchants and the kingdoms in the interior was carried on by African "middlemen." The erudite Arab Al Mas'udi from Bagdad supplied us with the first details about those coastal people and the trade in the early 10th century AD. We learn from him that they wore exclusively iron ornaments and that the African elephant tusks were sent almost exclusively via Oman to China and India. In the late 10th century there is already evidence from the Limpopo city states of a thriving trade in worked ivory, the most common objects being bracelets. Those Afro-Arabian centuries apparently favored the development of African crafts, while the Afro-European centuries contributed to their decline when they could not compete with the cheap import of industrial products.

The 12th century brought a change which contributed to the decline of the Limpopo city states. A dynasty of sultans was established at Kilwa, transforming the city into a prosperous Islamic port and seeking out sources for gold. This new trade brought wealth to the kingdom of Zimbabwe whose heartland was the high plateau between the Limpopo and Zambesi rivers. The kings of Zimbabwe controlled a sophisticated network that linked villages and cities within the state, and the state itself with the trans-Oceanic trade. The foreign goods that have been excavated in Zimbabwe comprised such luxury goods as Chinese Celadon dishes, glazed stoneware from the Far East, Persian fayence bowls, and Indian glass beads. In addition, Chinese records of the 13th century confirm that

A bronze courtier from the Kingdom of Benin, Nigeria, sixteenth to seventeenth century (Courtesy of Städtisches Museum Braunschweig). The courtier wears the same type of bugle beads around his neck as the members of the royal family, yet in a smaller quantity.

silks and fine cottons were reckoned among the goods exported to East Africa. Kilwa and Great Zimbabwe developed a mutually beneficial partnership, with both exchanging quite standard goods in their own economies. Just as glass beads and porcelain were "industrial" products, gold was easily acquired by the African rulers as tribute.

In the northern world, gold was the instrument of power, while in those early centuries in Africa the possession of such exotica as glass beads conferred equally power and a high rank within the social hierarchy. As even today we maintain the artificially high value of gold by a strictly limited distribution, African rulers controlled the access to such foreign goods as glass beads - and thus they were generally only found in those medieval city states in the very wealthy districts - along with copper, iron, and gold ornaments.

## "Glaze Kambaysche Kralen" (=Cambayan glass beads)
## (Olfert Dappert, 1668)

Indian glass bead production started in antiquity, with the oldest excavated glass beads dating back to about 1000 BC. Glass beads have been found in archeological sites in the area of ancient trade centers and on a side branch of the ancient trans-Asian trade route, such as in the area of Mathura/India, where the beads date back to about 800 BC and in Taxila near modern Islamabad in Pakistan, where the beads date back to the 6th century BC. Other important bead industries grew and apparently worked in connection with the trans-Oceanic trade which was considerably intensified in the period of the Roman Empire. Industries have been located in the south of India, on the western side south of Bombay, with beads dating back to the Roman Empire, and on the eastern side south of Madras with beads dating back to medieval times. Since at least Hellenistic periods these beads were drawn beads in various sizes - sometimes as small as 3 mm in diameter - and in many shades, such as yellow, orange, red, violet, blue, green, and black in transparent as well as in opaque glass.

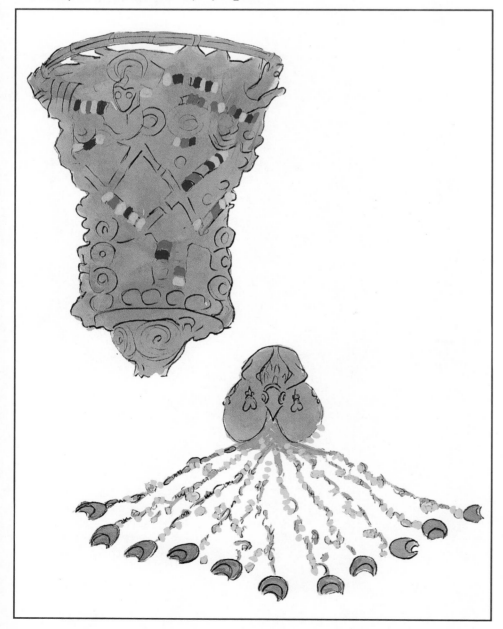

Sketch of a bronze ornament and a bronze pendant from Nigeria, 9th/10th century (both items are in the collection of the National Museum Lagos, Nigeria). The ornament was encrusted all over with glass beads which were attached with wire to the ornament. The beaded decoration underlined the pattern of the metallic design. The few remaining beads are blue, red, and yellow. The beads are drawn and wound beads. Some of the drawn beads had been cut from multisided canes. Some among the beads are additionally faceted and some are overlay beads. The bronze pendants consist of two eggs upon which a bird is stretched protectively. Each egg is decorated with three bronze flies. Below the eggs are attached eleven bronze chains which end upon bells and which are decorated with opaque yellow glass beads.

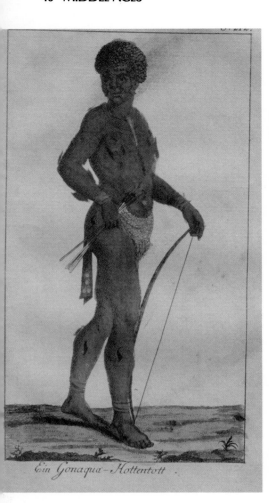

*Ein Gonaqua - Hottentott.*

A South African in the eighteenth century. The South Africans were, according to Dutch reports of the sixteenth and seventeenth centuries, among the first Africans who substituted their locally made copper beads for glass beads from India. They traditionally created elaborate beadwork on their skin dresses with copper beads in yellow and red shades.

A necklace with millefiori beads from Murano, 1920s and 1930s. In the background a glass fragment which is attributed to the ninth century AD is visible. Similar cane patterns appear for the first time on Egyptian mosaic glass of the Hellenistic period (second century BC to first century AD). Such millefiori beads have been a great success on the African market in modern times.

The old texts don't mention any of these places but refer repeatedly to a manufacturing center in the Gulf of Cambay - a region which is generally only associated with the Indian stone bead industry.

In the "Periplous of the Erythraean Sea" which dates back to the 1st century AD, we already find indications that Egyptian and possibly Arabian raw glass was exported to Barygaza - situated in the Gulf of Cambay - and to various ports in south India.[1]

Around 1500 the royal commercial agent Duarte Barboza from Portugal reported that small glass beads in grey (probably made from low-quality clear glass), red, and yellow came from "the great kingdom of Cambay" and were bartered in Sofala on the east African coast to the African merchants. From "the voyage and travell of M. Caesar Fredericke, marchant of Venice" in the years 1563-1581 we have the following report:

> *From Chaul they trade along the coast of Melinde in Ethiopia (=Africa) within the land of Cafraria: on that coast are many good harbors kept by the Moores. Tither the Portugals bring a kind of Bombast cloth of a low price, and great store of Paternosters or beads made of paltrie glasse, which they make in Chaul according to the use of the countrey: and from thence they cary Elephants teeth for India, slaves called Cafari, and some amber and gold.[2]*

English navigational handbooks of the 16th century indicate the "Chaul" was located in the Gulf of Cambay north of Bombay. This Cambayan provenance of the glass beads is confirmed again by the Dutch records of the 17th century.

[1]Stern, 1985:33
[2]Hakluyt, vol. III, no date:264-265

Cylindrical beads from India, uncertain period, possibly early 20th century. These beads represent a classical shape and size (5-8mm length) of Indian beads. The Muranese as well as the Bohemian bead industries took up this pattern and the European "porcelain" beads finally subplanted any type of those "filler" beads.

A necklace with modern millefiori beads from India. The same areas which had a near monopoly of the African bead trade in the Middle Ages are currently producing imaginative lampworked beads "in the Venetian manner" for the fashionable European market and the African market as well.

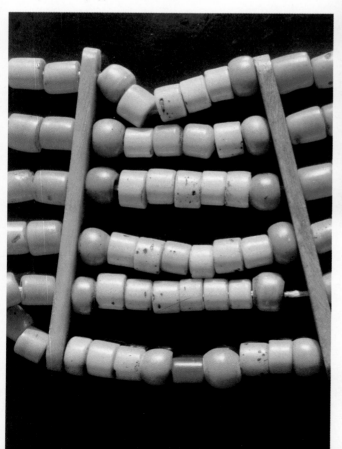

Elaborate modern beads from Java. Southeast Asia has had links with East Africa since antiquity, and glass beads may have been a commodity in this ancient trading contact. Some of the finest and most imaginative glass beads available today are being made in Java.

Cylindrical and round beads from India, possibly early 20th century. These cylindrical beads look at first sight like drawn beads yet they are wound beads.

# EUROPEAN BEAD INDUSTRIES

## Beads From the Bavarian and Bohemian Forest

Dozens of beadmaking glassworks took up production after 1500 in the Bavarian/Bohemian Forest. Four such "Paternoster" works were founded soon after 1500 within the boundaries of a single Bohemian feudal estate. The beadmaking works Hirschschlag, not far away from the glassworks Frauenau (see page 31), began its beadmaking in 1545 and the glassworks Breitenau, close to Bischofsmais/Bavarian Forest, started the production of glass buttons and -ringlets for rosaries in 1585.[1] The mathematician and geographer Philipp Appian (1531-1589) reported from one of the many paternosterworks in Bavaria in the 1550s:

> They produce the little globes that are meant for counting prayers in a great variety of sizes and shapes. A single worker produces per day many thousands of such vitreous globules - even up to 30,000 and more.[2]

This enormous figure - which should be reliable as it comes from a mathematician - allows for the conclusion that the Bavarian paternosterworks produced (among other possible types of beads) already drawn beads at this period. The daily output of a beadmaker in wound beads was, according to many records throughout the centuries, between 6,000 and 18,000; in blown beads between 4,000 and 6,000, while a record of the 20th century says that an excellent beadcutter was able to produce 60,000 "Sprengperlen" per day.[3]

Records from the first years of the 17th century confirm that almost every possible basic type of bead was produced in this area, including wound beads, drawn beads, faceted beads, and molded beads. Some of those beads were explicitly paternoster beads, and thus were probably at least pea-sized, but some among them were very small beads. Among the recorded bead deliveries to Nuremberg the bead colors blue and black dominate, but they also were comprised of white, yellow, and green beads. Quite mystifying is the reference to a certain type of beads named "Schiller."[4] This specific type is always more expensive than the other types. The term "Schiller" - which in modern German would be translated with "luster" or "iridescence" - seems to indicate an iridescent surface, while the written context and the study of further sources from this period suggest rather that these beads had an agate-like appearance, comparable to the Italian "calcedonio." This glass variety was apparently much appreciated for beads in this period. The Muranese beadmakers were not the only ones to make such beads, the beadmakers in Pisa did as well.[5]

We learn from a collection of "business" letters that in the years 1604-1610 those types of beads were sent from seven different glassworks - some of which had already existed in the mid-16th century - to three merchants in Nuremberg.[6] The merchants delivered on their turn such raw materials as manganese and cobalt to the glassmakers as well as the necessary tools for reducing the glass (canes) into beads. They sent large quantities of grindstones which points to the high amount of drawn/cut beads. The beads were packed in bags and/or delivered in wooden barrels. From Nuremberg they were traded either to Amsterdam (for the African trade of the European merchants) or into "Turkey" (for the African trade of the Arab merchants). "Turkey," in the German sources of this period, meant the Ottoman Empire which had comprised, since about 1500, not only modern Turkey but also the larger part of the Balkan region and Greece, and since about the mid-16th century, also contained Syria and the North African coast. It is most likely that this well-established trade from Nuremberg into "Turkey," which went via Venice, created contact between the bead industries in the Bavarian/Bohemian Forest and the Muranese glassworks producing glass canes. It seems the Nuremberg merchants were extremely successful in marketing the Bavarian beads, as the letters of the makers include repeated excuses for not supplying enough beads. It was most likely the high demand for these beads which induced the merchants to use foreign glass canes as well. The demand for these Bavarian beads around 1600 was already so very high that the makers worked year-round without interruption. The Muranese complained about "i tedeschi" (=the Germans) in the early 16th century, because they traded Muranese canes to Germany in order to reduce them into beads.[7] Those "Germans" were most likely such merchants from Nuremberg (or Regensburg) which supplied their makers in the Bavarian/Bohemian Forest with additional semi-finished material for making a sufficient amount of beads. We lack any conclusive evidence that the Muranese canes traded into "Germany" arrived in the Bavarian/Bohemian Forest, but there was hardly any other important glassmaking region north of the Alps which was equally experienced in making the various types of beads, because most among them had specialized in other types of glass. Alsace-Lorraine, for example, had concentrated on mirror-making since the 14th century, and the glassmakers in the Spessart Forest were above all experts in blown and window glass. The recorded glass beadmakers in 16th century Nuremberg can be more or less excluded from working the Muranese canes because this would have been reflected in the Nuremberg guild records.

[1] Blau, 1941:90
[2] Sellner, 1988:18
[3] Stahl, 1926:155
[4] Blau, 1941:94/95
[5] Zecchin I, 1987:172
[6] Blau, 1941:92-96
[7] Zecchin II, 1989:205/206

## "Müller" beads

The ever rising importance of this bead industry is documented by the start of many further beadmaking glassworks in the 17th and 18th century, and its eminent role is confirmed by the fact that even the most famous among the makers of this area - the glassmaster Michael Müll(n)er (1639-1709), to whom the "invention" of the Bohemian crystal is attributed - entered the bead business around 1680.

We don't know for sure which types of beads he made. As he is said to have "improved" beadmaking, we might dismiss the possibility that he made simple wound beads, as their making has remained almost unchanged from antiquity until modern times. As Müllers glassworks - the "Helmbacher Hütte" - reckoned among the best glassworks of Bohemia, he certainly concentrated on the "better" varieties of beads. He supplied the glass engravers and cutters of North Bohemia with his Bohemian crystal, yet he also marketed finished products directly to foreign countries such as Italy, Spain, "Turkey," and above all, to the Netherlands from where it was traded worldwide.[1] His beads were delivered to Frankfurt and Strassburg and these destinations allow for the conclusion that he did not produce beads for the trade to Africa and America, but for the fashionable European market - which means mainly artificial pearls, i.e. blown beads.

Many glassworks of this area extended their production to blown glass during the 18th century as well, but beadmaking remained a leading

A German woodcut depicting a patrician bride from Nuremberg with abundant beadwork on her bridal headpiece. Such urban and upper class fashions and ornaments were soon adopted by the wealthy rural population and the urban middle class. They copied the patterns yet used (instead of precious beads and pearls) less valuable beads made of organic materials and of glass.

A German woodcut from Augsburg, 1508, depicting pilgrims, almost all wearing a rosary. Important Catholic cities like Nuremberg, Regensburg, Augsburg, and many more in Southern Germany were meeting points for thousands of pilgrims. Thus, for traders and craftsmen, incentives for the production of rosary beads were strong.

production line. Thus, we learn of a standard glassworks which produced "little mirrors and glass beads for bartering in the slave trade" that employed two glassblowers and twenty-two beadmakers in 1717.[2]

German as well as Italian sources of the 18th century confirm that the demand for glass beads rose to unknown heights during this century. This bead boom had negative consequences for the Bavarian/Bohemian producers as well as the Muranese/Venetian beadmakers. While those beadmakers had to cope with the burden of traditions which prevented an adequate response to the new market situation, the younger bead industries in Thuringia and North Bohemia rose to successful competitors.

[1]Barta, 1936:161
[2]Mares, 1893:105

I. Mahlschatz: Halskette aus zusammengedrückten Mariengroschen und Korallen (etwas verkleinert)

A necklace and two brooches with Bavarian-style beads made by Iangani in Germany in the 1960s. This type of furnace-wound bead became the standard bead from Bavaria in the nineteenth century, yet in previous periods the beadmakers from the Bavarian Forest had produced almost any type of glass beads which were requested on the market. Since the nineteenth century, however, they have had difficulty withstanding competition from the North Bohemian beadmakers and therefore reduced their range of beads. During the early twentieth century, the furnace-wound beads were not appreciated any longer, but Bavarian wound beads enjoyed a splendid revival in the 1950s through the fashion jewelry artist Anni Schaad-Lang from Stuttgart.

A necklace composed of coral and folded coins made in Germany in the seventeenth or eighteenth century. Jewelry of this type for use with regional dress (costumes) determined the design and size of glass beads. The most frequently found beads in this type of jewelry are amber, coral, garnet, and glass.

German woodcut of the sixteenth century depicting a lady from Augsburg wearing her customary rosary. The rosaries were the only piece of jewelry which escaped the rigid costume laws in Europe for long periods.

Various "stone" beads and among them some larger agate-colored beads, uncertain origin and period, probably Bohemia. Agate-colored beads were throughout the history of European beadmaking a most appreciated variety of glassbeads. Venetian "calcedonio" beads were made since the late 15th century and the Bavarian "Schiller" beads of the early 17th century were most likely such beads as well.

Strands of blown glass faux "pearls" from Bavaria and Bohemia from the early twentieth century. The glass beads which the famous glass master Michael Müller from the Bohemian Forest produced in the late seventeenth century were most likely artificial pearls. He delivered his beads to the fashion capitals in Europe in the same way as the beads in this picture were sold to Paris where they received their seller's label.

## Beads and the Baroviers

The Muranese makers entered the bead business in the second half of the 15th century with the production of glass canes. In fact, it was but a single family - the famous Baroviers - which is recorded to have produced canes by the 15th century and which made negative publicity in 1469/70 with this new production line. Taddeo Barovier (died in 1480) was accused of having circumvented the guild laws and the imposed annual closure of the glassworks by dislocating production to Ancona (circa 250 km south of Venice on the coast) and selling glass canes to Syria.[1]

Considering the medieval bead trade of the Arab merchants to Africa, and judging by the patterns of the compound canes from Murano, there can be little doubt that the Baroviers had started to supply the Afro-Arabian bead trade with such deliveries. The economical disturbances in the African trade of the Arab merchants - caused by the Genoese trading monopoly on the north African coast always extending further east (including even Egypt around 1400), and by the Portuguese, who had begun to compete with the Arabs on the lucrative West African market since about the mid-15th century - combined with the loss of possible bead suppliers when the Mongols extended their Empire as far as to include the region of modern Iraq, might have induced the Arabian merchants to look for new suppliers. Yet it is equally possible that the Baroviers had become aware themselves of this promising market - as the early Baroviers, beginning with the famous Angelo, were apparently not only excellent glass makers, but keen businessmen as well.

Their success on the market was possibly further ensured because they offered better quality. Compound canes and beads had long since been in production - yet the Baroviers were possibly the first to practice mold-shaping to achieve the pointed pattern within their Rosetta canes. Such shaping in crenelated molds is recorded in European glass industries since about the 13th century.[2] The use of this procedure for making multicolored overlay canes was certainly a most important step forward in the matter of productivity and quality.

By the 1490s the Baroviers had been drawing their excellent canes from monochrome crystal and overlay glass for twenty-five years. Beads were also made out of such canes, but seemingly on rather small scale, for wherever such "drawn" beads appear in the 15th century records they are quoted in single beads! At this time, we were still far away from a flourishing bead industry. Several reasons might account for this:

- The necessary know-how for reducing the canes into beads had not yet been properly rooted in Murano.

- The Barovier family lacked a strong business personality - as the outstanding Marino Barovier had died in 1485 and the family seems to have suffered from internal discord, if not litigation, in the 1490s. Yet Marino had at least taken care of 1482s addendum to the mariegola - the guild regulations - guaranteeing that the making of certain beads out of the Muranese canes should not become a Venetian profession but should remain a privilege of the Muranese makers.[3]

- The other Muranese makers had apparently not yet entered this production line, either because they lacked the necessary technological knowledge, or because they hadn't yet perceived the economical potential of canes and drawn beads.

Giorgio Ballarin (circa 1440 - 1506), whose family had immigrated from Dalmatia, is the only recorded maker to become truly involved in beadmaking shortly before 1500. He attracted two German beadcutters to Murano where they reduced canes into beads in his factory.[4]

[1]Zecchin I, 1987:55 and Zecchin II, 1989:210
[2]Baumgarther, 1988:28ff

[3]Zecchin I, 1987:58
[4]Zecchin II, 1989:205

## "Paternostri" and "Oldani"

On the occasion of Marino's initiatives in 1482 we learn about definite types of drawn beads. "Paternostri cristalini" and "Oldani" are recorded, both being clear glass beads, while the equally mentioned "Paternostri a rosete" were basically the famous Rosetta beads. From a Barovier inventory of 1496 we learn of two beadcolors; light blue and "calcedonio" (=agate-colored), and of oval beads ("Ulivette") and twisted cylindrical beads ("Paternostri voltadi").[1]

Only in 1511 did the Muranese makers seem to finally rise out from their inertness in the bead business with an official complaint about the German merchants who were making the beads, and the profits, out of their canes. These glass masters now showed every possible determination to take bead production into their own hands, yet even in 1525, at least part of the Rosetta canes and possibly other canes as well were still being reduced into beads in Germany and continued to be traded via the "Fondaco dei Tedeschi" in Venice towards the Levante.[2]

The greatest impediment to a successful bead production was probably the guild bureaucracy. The elaborate guild system, which tried to satisfy and protect the interests of so many different makers, had split the various types and steps of beadmaking into different groups of craftsmen. The Venetian "veriselli" would be able to cast/mold, and possibly wind, certain beads - but not to cut them. The Venetian "cristalleri" were allowed to cut the beads, which they got possibly as pre-shaped beads from the "veriselli" - but not to shape them in any other way. And certain Muranese "vetrai" (glassmakers) - but not every Muranese glassmaker - were allowed to draw canes and to reduce them into special types of beads. As regards the reduction of the canes into beads, they had to be careful not to infringe upon the beadmaking rights of the "cristalleri." The many prohibitive rules and the institutionalized system of denunciation which were meant to keep the industry together were, in fact, a hindrance to the progress which resulted instead from competition between Muranese and Venetian makers and the immigrants who enriched the local glass and bead business on a constant basis.

[1]Zecchin II, 1989:212
[2]Cristalleri:52

## "Canelle" and "Spollete"

When the Muranese makers expressed their determination to intensify bead production in 1511, their plans relied upon the bead varieties which they had learned through German merchants. Thus, they intended to do "paternostri curti e longhi, canelle et spollete,"[1] which means globular and oblong (faceted) beads, cylindrical beads, and oval beads. In addition, we learn from the Siennese Vanuccio Biringuccio that the Muranese produced a variety of beads in the 1530s which was possibly made from filigree canes. I interpret the description "con gli avoltichiamenti di ruschi" in such a way, since the making of sophisticated blown filigree glass had just been launched in 1527.

Meanwhile, cane drawing had spread among Muranese makers. Their successful production was supported by a collection of recipes, which had existed since at least 1523, and which dealt exclusively with the proper mixture of constituents for obtaining glass suitable for drawing canes.[2] Cane drawing was perfected in such a way as to allow a cane length of about 15-20 meters.[3]

The Venetian beadmakers continued to produce their yellow faceted beads. There is further evidence of this specific variety in a Venetian inven-

Rosetta beads from Murano, different but uncertain periods.
(Thomas Morbe, Frankfurt) "There are some dark blue and red beads...which are obviously of modern make. They have been cut from a glass cane in which a white line with twelve starlike points divides the red center from the blue outer coating. These beads are widely scattered over the world; in 1848 some were found in Keswick, one comes from Dakkah, Egypt, and other places; it has been suggested that they are early Venetian, and the star alludes to the twelve appostles." (Wallace-Dunlop, 19th century: 206)

The selection of glass beads which existed according to the written soures around the late 15th/early 16th century in Murano and Venice. We have written evidence for the naming of the beads but no beads which can be attributed without doubt to this early period yet there remain only a few uncertainties about their basic shapes. The cylindrical beads are in fact nothing but a short cane - hence the name "canella." "Ulivetta" (=olive) and "spoletta" (=spool) are two designations which point clearly to the oval shape. The faceted or rounded "patemostri" correspond to the standard shapes of rosary beads made from rock crystal. The possible shape of the "oldani" bead corresponds to a proposal of Luigi Zecchin and the possible shape of the "paternostro voltado" is my proposal which is based on the design of known antique beads and more recent beads. It was most likely an oblong twisted bead which was cut from a four or multi-sided cane.

A necklace including millefiori beads, Murano, 1920s. The background shows polychrome Islamic glass fragments from about the 9th century AD. These fragments have similar patterns and colors as the beads on the necklace. This glass design line had been created in ancient Egypt. Such extremely colorful millefiori beads had been created for the African market since about the late nineteenth century. They became fashionable on the European market since the 1920s.

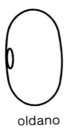

oldano

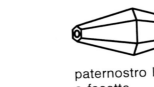

paternostro lungo
a facette

canella

paternostro (curto)

ulivetta
spolleta

paternostro (curto)
a facette

paternostro
voltado

tory of 1528,[4] and some recipes of 1536 which are based upon Muranese glass technology comprise a recipe for making yellow lead glass suitable for beads.[5] It is the only bead-related recipe in this collection. This "Ricettario di Montpellier" also refers to the making of knife handles, and in the corresponding recipes we learn indirectly about furnace winding/"lampworking" overlay beads, on which a core is covered with crushed glass.[6]

    There is no doubt that the Muranese and Venetian beadmakers were already producing excellent - if not to say unequalled - beads during the 16th century. The isolated beadmakers in the forests north of the Alps (mass) produced for markets unknown to them and relied on nothing but inspiration from the merchants while the Muranese and Venetian beadmakers were creating in a much more inspiring context. Yet there is no evidence that they dominated the "big" bead market in the way they have succeeded since the late 18th century. This was most likely caused by the dramatic upheavals which have changed world (trade) since the early 16th century.

    Christopher Columbus had initiated European exploitation of the Americas in 1492, and since 1498, Vasco da Gama had made it possible to destroy the Venetian and Arabian monopoly in the lucrative Euro-Oriental trade. The Mediterranean, which had been the "central square" of the world trade, became a waterway of secondary importance in the coming century. Almost overnight, Venice lost its central position in the world trade and was not prepared for the new challenges. The loss of its colonial empire - beginning with the loss of Cyprus in 1571 and ending in 1718 with the peace treaty of Passarovitz, completed Venetian degradation as a trading capital. Its withdrawal from the business scene did not affect its eminence as a cultural focal point, however.

[1] Zecchin II, 1989:40
[2] ibid.:330
[3] Biringuccio, 1540:
[4] Zecchin I, 1987:173
[5] ibid.:258
[6] ibid.:264

An African fetish adorned with cylindrical beads. This shape of beads was apparently much appreciated in Africa and became one of the standard bead shapes in the bead trade from Europe to Africa.

*Opposite page, bottom right:*
A vase including Rosetta slices, Murano, 1992. This is a modern and artistic interpretation of the classical mosaic glass theme.

Green compound beads of the E. Moretti & f.lli company from Murano, twentieth century, and a strand of lampworked beads including similar cane segments, Murano, 1920s. The beads are arranged upon a background showing glass fragments of the 9th century AD, including striped cane segments of a similar pattern.

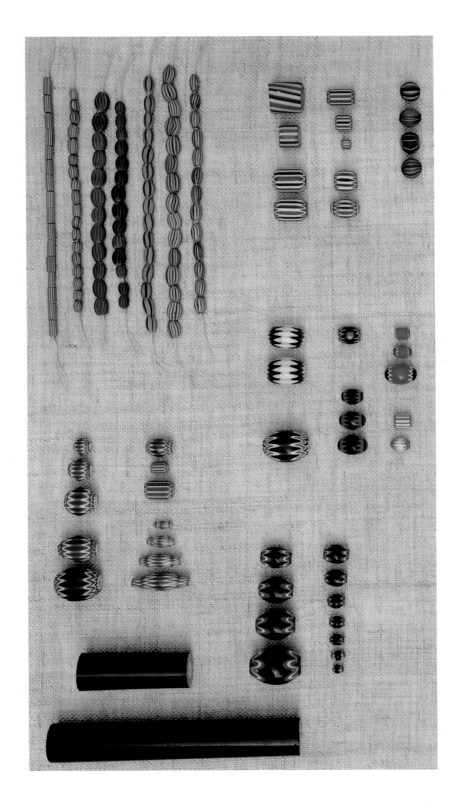

A sample card with various types of Rosetta beads and striped beads, E. Moretti & f.lli, Murano, twentieth century (Courtesy of E. Moretti & f.lli). Already the Muranese makers of the 16th century offered not only the famous blue Rosetta bead but also other such overlay beads in various color combinations.

# Expansion and "Espatrio" (=Emigration)

Muranese and Venetian bead "industries" had apparently begun to flourish in the 16th century - yet the beadmakers have suffered since this century from not only external blows, but also from internal sclerosis. The established glass dynasties, well pampered by the guild laws, tried everything to prevent "disturbances" from newcomers. They did not always succeed, however, as in the case of Giorgio Ballarin, who caused a lot of turmoil around 1500, but who eventually advanced the Muranese bead business considerably (he was apparently a decisive promoter in transforming the Muranese cane industry into a proper bead industry). The glass masters became equally conservative after coming "into power" in 1544. The "padroni" - the owners of the glassworks - had been the strongest members in the guilds until this time as they held the "secreti"; the knowledge about the precious glass recipes. But the "maestri" - the glass masters - had perfected the world-renowned "Venetian" glass design, and thus were now the bearers of Venetian glass fame. Twenty-three new articles in the mariegola - added onto the Doge's initiative in 1544 - accounted for this. The loss of freedom for the glass masters, as they were strictly forbidden to emigrate, was counterbalanced by a leading role in the guilds' administration and complete social security, which was the charge of the "padroni." Since medieval time, the emigration of qualified craftsmen had been a standard regulatory principle in Europe to avoid undue local competition. Because of these new rules, Murano soon suffered from an overabundance of glass masters which became a burden upon the "padroni." At first, the problem was attempted to be solved by increasing the difficulty of the examinations required to become a glass master, and later, in 1689 and 1720, the exams were discontinued for a period of five to ten years.[1]

[1]Barovier-Mentasti, 1982:134

## "Perle"

Throughout 16th century Europe it became almost an obsession to create all kinds of artificial pearls. The attempts and research which resulted were reactions to an ever growing demand for affordable pearls, as the customary gold ornamentation in upper-class fashions were suddenly considered to be demoded, and, as in the 1560s, "pearl" ornaments became a "must." The substitutes created for expensive oriental pearls were composed according to various methods - and the European glassmakers took up the challenge as well.

Since about the second half of the 16th century, the diversity of Venetian glass beads had been enriched by the bead varieties of the lampworkers/beadblowers. Whether "lampworking" had grown from existing "small work" - such as gemmaking in Venice, or working with a small furnace (as we know from Maria Barovier in 15th century Murano) - or whether it had been an imported craft, the competition of the free lampworkers which had begun to create glass beads became such a nuisance to beadmakers with corporate status in the early 17th century, that they forced the lampworkers to join the beadmakers guild in 1629. This enforced alliance survived only twenty years. "Pearl" production soon became such an important production line that the lampworkers were able to organize separately in 1648. The beadblowing required a different type of cane and thus we find, for the first time in the records of the 17th century, specialists for drawing "canna da perle" (=tubes for blown beads).[1] As the sheen of the finest "pearls" depended largely upon the type of glass, before the end of the 17th century the Muranese had created their famous "girasole," a slightly opalescent glass. [2]

A view of Venice in the 17th/eighteenth century.

"Girasole" was used for creating art glass as well but became famous throughout Europe as the ideal glass for making artificial pearls.

It was not only the lampworkers of the "Serenissima" who cared about "pearl"making, but many other European beadmakers did as well. Foreign competition was considered a severe threat in Venice and it was strictly forbidden to export any glass which might be useful to others in making fine "pearls."[3]

[1]Zecchin II, 1989:120
[2]Zecchin, 1986:63
[3]Cristalleri:138ff.

## "Paternostri a speo" and "Paternostri a ferrazza"

The "paternostreri" - the beadmakers - were originally beadcutters, and thus belonged to the cutters guild or the "cristalleri," cutting rock crystal and later glass as well. In the beginning, they probably cut beads (and gems) which came from the Venetian gemmakers, but with the supply of glass canes from Murano in the 16th century, their profession took a new turn. Originally, the canes were just cut into beads with the large beads being further cut and ground at the ends and the small beads eventually tumbled with an abrasive to smooth down the ends, but at some stage in the 16th century, the larger cane segments were arranged upon a spit and further shaped and rounded by reheating. This working of beads "a speo" - on a spit - is one of many technical terms which led to a lot of misinterpretation. Beads which were worked "a speo" were not necessarily wound or lampworked beads in the

Lampworked figurines of the glass artist Lucio Bubacco from Venice, 1990. "Suppia lume" (=lamp work) means not necessarily beadmaking. In the 16th century it meant primarily fancy lampworking and creating such figurines and similar items. Only in the 17th century the lampworkers started beadmaking on a larger scale and thus infringed upon the rights of the beadmakers - the "paternostreri" - with corporate status.

modern sense of the terms. Up to the 18th century, the expression refers rather to a final shaping of cane segments which had been aligned upon a spit and rounded by reheating.

It is not recorded exactly what happened when during the 16th century, but towards the end of the century this major branch of beadmaking had split into two branches:

- The customary making of drawn beads which were finished by heating them upon an iron spit ("paternostri a speo").

-The making of drawn beads which were finished by reheating them in a kind of large pan to smoothen the rough end ("paternostri a ferrazza"). Judging by some records,[1] the pan-procedure was possibly introduced shortly before 1600. This simplification in finishing the beads and thus achieving a greater output was possibly developed in response to a rising demand for mass-produced European glass beads, suitable to supplant the Indian glass beads on the African market. The pan-beads were not necessarily very small beads but could well have the size of spit-beads. The finishing upon the spit produced better beads, but it was far more time-consuming.

In the early 17th century we find plenty of references referring to the differentiation between spit-beads and pan-beads. This might be a further indication that the pan-procedure had only recently been introduced. In 1613, the "Mariegola" includes for the first time precise data about the necessary exams for becoming either "maestro a ferrazza" - master in making pan-beads - or "maestro a spe(d)o" - master for making spit-beads.[2]

[1]Cristalleri:409
[2]ibid.:80/81

## The Muranese makers and their beads

Controversy between the Venetian and the Muranese makers had been a major reason why the Muranese had fought for their privilege to work certain types of beads out of their canes in the early 16th century. One hundred years later, in 1612, this privilege was once again confirmed - but at the same time the Muranese were asked to ensure an ever sufficient supply of canes to the Venetian beadmakers![1] The latent disagreements between those two groups of craftsmen soon became a secondary problem. The rising demand for beads and thus for canes put another pressure upon the Muranese cane industry: everybody wanted to become "maestro da canna" - cane master. Local competition grew unbearably high and the cane quality dropped to a new low. In an attempt to deal with this problem, access to mastery was made more difficult and starting in 1667 the cane drawers had to pass a specific exam to become a cane master.[2] They had to draw a multisided(?) cane for pan-work and a striped cane (white with red stripes) for spit-work.

The rapidly increasing demand for glass beads couldn't prevent an ever growing loss of qualified glassmakers and beadmakers. Once European glassmakers had fled the restrictions of their respective countries and become drawn to the flourishing capital of Venice, for similar reasons local makers began to feel the attraction towards new focal points in Europe.

[1]Zecchin II, 1989:46
[2]ibid.:110

Drawn beads of uncertain origin and period. The "paternostri a ferrazza," the mass-produced drawn beads of the 17th century, on which the finishing work had been considerably simplified by reheating simultaneously great quantities of beads in a kind of pan, were not necessarily small beads! The "maestri a ferrazza" - the beadmakers working with a pan - made basically two types of beads and one type was quite large! Those larger beads might have looked like these beads.

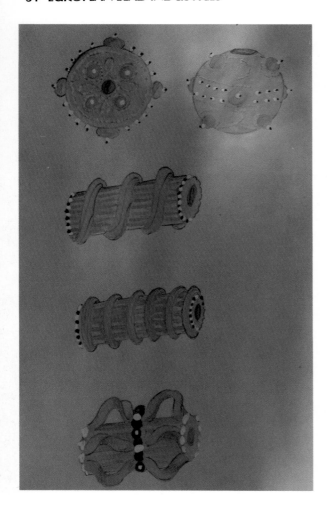

Sketches of lampworked beads possibly from Venice, 16th/17th century.
The string including these extraordinary beads was in the Ducal collection the castle Ambras, Innsbruck. It is now in the collection of the Museum für Angewandte Kunst (MAK) in Vienna.
The string includes additionally round beads which are blown from clear crystal.
The beads depicted here are gold-coated. The round beads are blown and further decorated with thin trailings and with dots which are made from white and blue glass.
The oblong beads have a solid core which consists of a crenelated cane segment. This cylinder is entwined with a thinner crenelated cane. The ends are decorated with white and blue glass dots.
A further variety of oblong beads has a similar cylindrical core which is further decorated with loops of a twisted and four-sided cane. These beads are equally decorated with white and blue glass dots.
This necklace proves that early lampworked beads looked eventually quite different from the lampworked beads with which we are familiar - most types of which have been designed in the late eighteenth/early nineteenth century. Yet these beads belonged to a ducal collection and the standard lampworked beads of that period were certainly less sophisticated.

"Margaritine" from Murano and Gablonz, 1930s. Since the 16th century the term "margarite" had been applied by European merchants to glass beads. This designation had possibly been introduced by Portuguese traders. Since the 17th century it was used in Venice as a general term for (drawn) beads and the small "margarite" were named "margaritine."

Aventurine beads of the E. Moretti & f.lli company from Murano, 1930s to 1950s. The glittery glass variety named "aventurine" had been created around 1644 in Murano. The first such beads were made in the 17th century as well.

A necklace including flat aventurine elements, India, late nineteenth/early twentieth century. The sparkling aventurine from Murano was highly estimated in Asia. It was exported in large pieces and worked into beads or similar elements in the respective countries. Presently, aventurine is made in Asian glass industries as well.

## "Conterie"

Records about Muranese and Venetian beadmaking up to the 18th century are anything but plentiful and precise, but the second half of the 18th century brings plenty of detailed information.

The information about specific bead types in the first half of the 18th century are still quite scarce - possibly because (mass) production was not yet very diversified. It was a period in which the makers suffered from a rising demand that could not adequately be met due to local production structures, which were too rigid to adapt (see "How to Improve the Bead Trade"). Thus major competing industries sprang up in Austria, France, and Germany, while the entire local industry was suffering from stagnation. The Venetians blamed these new foreign glass and bead industries for their own homemade economic difficulties, and so the administration, in a further vain attempt to support local industry, prohibited all trade with foreign glass in 1720!

Some farsighted glassmakers had tried to improve the inner structure of the bead industry since the early 18th century, but any innovative attempt such as unification within a bead-cooperative to prevent self-destructive local competition was "successfully" rebuffed by the bead-establishment. Finally, in 1763, when the loss of qualified workers and profits had become unbearable, it was decided to fundamentally revise the "mariegole" of the various glassmaking branches.

The larger part of the 18th century seems to have brought no major changes regarding the bead design of mass-produced beads. The makers

Beadwork necklace from Bohemia, 1920s. Beadwork with glass beads was an exclusive craft up to the 16th century and became a widespread fashionable craft in Europe since the 17th century. Necklaces and rosaries composed of tiny beads and including beaded beads belonged, since this time, to the standard beadwork. But as those early beadwork necklaces were strung on cotton they broke easily and hardly any have survived.

Advertisement of the merchant/manufacturer of lampworked beads Bernardo Rossi, Venice, who entered business in 1792 (Courtesy of State Archives of Venice). The gilded blown beads are explicitly mentioned on this advertisement.

Advertisement of the merchant/manufacturer of lampworked beads Gasparo Gabotti, Venice, late eighteenth century (Courtesy of State Archives of Venice). The gilded blown beads are explicitly mentioned on this advertisement.

Advertisement of the merchant/manufacturer Ludovico Rubbi from Venice, who entered business in 1798 (Courtesy of State Archives of Venice). Flowered beads and gilded beads are explicitly mentioned on this advertisement. This manufacturer also offered a large range of artificial gemstones.

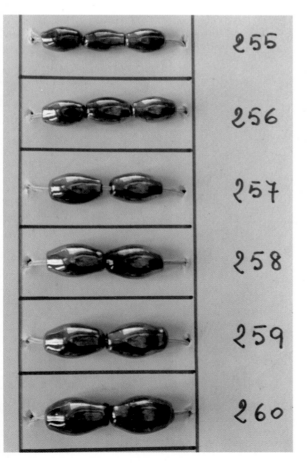

A sample card with bronze beads from Murano/Venice, nineteenth century (Glass Museum Murano). Similar bronze beads are recorded since the late eighteenth century. They became a tremendous success on the European market at least since the early nineteenth century. Bronze beads continued to be a most important production line yet modern bronze beads are mostly made in Neugablonz and in the Jablonec bead industry.

A sample card with lampworked beads from Murano/Venice, nineteenth century (Glass Museum Murano). The earliest known precisely dated lampworked beads from Murano/Venice are those on the Barbaria sample card (see pages 59-62) They allow us to assume that the lampworked "fiorate" (=flowered beads) which are mentioned on the advertisements of the late eighteenth century might have looked like the flowered beads on this sample card (numbers 291 and 292).

of spit-beads were fighting a losing battle against the makers of pan-beads, [1] and the only sophisticated spit-beads were apparently still the striped ones. [2] In 1766 the Muranese makers once again had their privilege to produce specific bead types confirmed, some of which were the Rosetta beads and other large beads which had to be "mezz' oncia almen di grossezza"; which means they had to have be at least 12 mm in diameter, [3] a rule which once again reflects the competition between Venetian and Muranese beadmakers. The major changes in the production of drawn beads were technological. The cane glass was perfected and fine new colors were created.

Traditional spit-working disappeared in the second half of the 18th century. By 1739, the spit-masters had already been invited to become "maestri a ferrazza," but their skills were presumably absorbed by the lampworkers guild since bead-lampworking had such a stupendous rise in the last third of the 18th century. The revision of the "mariegola" might have had its share in this but the recovery of the bead industry was also largely due to influence from foreign bead manufacturers and merchants (see "The Tyrolian Connection").

Forty-three woodcuts depicting the advertisements of Venetian bead manufacturers/merchants from the late 18th century provide us with detailed insight into the production of lampworked beads. Most of them only specify the production of gilded beads, which were obviously the main success on the market. The gilded beads of this period were neither foil beads, with gold inserted into layers of glass, nor were they lined with gold, but were covered with gold leaf according in a very time-consuming procedure. Six of these manufacturers also produced artificial corals - which were either blown beads lined with red, or lampworked beads with an "overlay" of crushed red glass. They produced "silver" beads which were either coated with silver foil in the same way as the "gold" beads, or lined with a metallic solution in the same way such beads were made in Bohemia and Thuringia. A further variety which was specifically mentioned was fancy blown beads - probably in various shapes and with various linings. For the first time, they also produced lampworked beads very similar to the lampworked beads we know today - with flowerlike decorations, trailings, and spatters - and, last but not least, they made bronze-colored beads.

[1]Margariteri:370 + 439
[2]Cecchetti, 1874:275
[3]ibid.:276

A sample card with lampworked beads from Murano/Venice, nineteenth century (Glass Museum Murano). These are again some types of beads which were presumably already offered in the second half of the eighteenth century. Amber-colored beads (number 362) are recorded since the 14th century. Striped drawn beads (number 356) had been on the market at least since the early 17th century. Aventurine beads (number 357) had been introduced in the 17th century. Ruby-red beads (numbers 360 and 361) had possibly been on the market since Orsella Mantovani was given in 1700 the permission to produce and sell ruby-red glass for making blown beads. Yet such thoroughly colored lampworked beads as on this sample card appeared most likely only in the late eighteenth century on the market. The fancy lampworked beads (numbers 358 and 359) represent two types which are included in the Barbaria sample card of 1815 but which were certainly made before the turn of the century as well.

## The Tyrolian Connection

During the 16th - 18th century, Tyrol was part of the Holy Roman Empire, comprised of a southern part of Tyrol which is now part of Italy. One of the most important trading routes connecting Nuremberg to Venice went right through Tyrol and its capital, Innsbruck. Thus this area had been very involved in various industries/crafts suitable for international trade since medieval times, and the area produced many versatile merchants. In the 18th century, Tyrol became a very controversial "partner" of the Venetian bead industry by attracting competent beadmakers from Murano and Venice but also enriching Venetian industry with competent makers/merchants.

Tyrolian beadmaking was decisively advanced, if not started, by the Archiduke Ferdinand of Tyrol (1529-1595). In the second half of the 16th century he began to promote various crafts within the ducal workshops where they produced perfect blown beads, as well as small beads, for beadwork. The craftsmen of the ducal workshops might well have acquired important skills in Murano and Venice - as the "padroni" in Murano continued to

Advertisement of the merchant/manufacturer Giorgio Barbaria from Venice, late eighteenth century (Courtesy of State Archives of Venice). G. Barbaria offers a huge selection of artificial gemstones and further lampworked items. He also offers blown beads lined with a silvery solution and made of glass in various colors.

GEORGIO BARBARIA Negoz.ᵀᴱ

*Tiene Fabrica di Rubini, Granate, Smalto, Mandole Schiette, e fioratte, Schizze con una, e tre Bisse, ossia righe, Pietre per Anelli, d'ogni Sorta di Colore, e grandezza Diamantade, e Schiette. Penachj di Vetro, Aghi da Pomolo con la Testa di Vetro Smaltada, e di più ogni altra Sorte di Mani-fattura di Vetro, e Smalto. E perle d'argento Bian.ᶜʰᵉ e Colorite.*

*ALL' INSEGNA DELLA NAVE BETTINA. La sua Abitazione, è in Calle lunga di Sᵗᵃ Mᵃ Formosa*
IN VENEZIA.

Sketch of two rosaries from the workshop of the Archiduke Ferdinand of Tyrol, 16th century. The rosaries are composed from blown beads, either with a red lining to simulate corals or with a fish-silver lining to simulate pearls. The gilded beads are not lined but coated with gold.

employ foreign workers and foreigners continued to settle in Murano and Venice, despite the many decrees in which the administration tried to prevent such foreign "intrusion."[1] The entire industry was actually invigorated by such an afflux of foreign talent, despite what the decrees - which were often dictated by the jealousy of the local establishment - may record.

We find no indication of any important emigration of local beadmakers to Innsbruck in the 16th century, while such "espatrio" is well recorded for the 18th century. This is generally described as a severe loss to local industry, but it must be admitted that this loss was largely caused by the sclerotic structure of the industry itself. For example, Gaetano Acquabona, who originated from Tyrol, became a lampworker in Venice and actively involved in the guild administration. Largely supported by young glassmakers, he tried to reform the administrative structure, causing such turmoil that he finally had to flee the country.[2] In 1766 he started a bead production in Innsbruck.[3] The Tyrolian family of Barbaria also had to fight local establishment in the beginning, yet they got along with them much better than Acquabona to become the most important manufacturers in the Venetian bead business. They coordinated local craftmanship and promoted Murano-Venetian beadmaking since the last twenty-five years of the 18th century to its highest level.

[1] Zecchin II, 1989:85-87
[2] Inquisitori di Stato, 826 (State Archives of Venice)
[3] Zecchin I, 1987:94

Some blown and gold-coated beads, possibly Venice, nineteenth century. These beads resemble closely the golden beads on the right rosary of the previous picture. They are extremely elaborate beads. They are blown into a perfect round shape, they have a carefully finished hole and the dotted trailings in clear crystal are applied with much regularity and care.

Blown coral beads from Gablonz, early twentieth century. These beads resemble closely the "corals" on the Ducal rosary. Blown "corals" reckoned like blown "pearls" among the earliest varieties in blown glass beads. Such blown coral beads were also offered by the Venetian manufacturers of the late eighteenth century.

## *The Ups and Downs of Modern Bead Production*

The beginning of the 19th century brought almost revolutionary changes to the bead industry:

- In 1806 the guild system was abolished.

- In 1817, the company Dalmistro, Moravia & Co. united all steps for making drawn beads under the roof of a single Muranese factory. Previously, the guild laws had split the various steps onto many different specialists in Venice as well as in Murano. This had been a huge impediment to high productivity.

- In addition, a rotary drum was introduced which had been developed by Luigi Pusinich. It replaced the customary pan for finishing drawn beads and caused an important rise in productivity.

- A range of entirely new glass colors was created and such famous glass varieties as the "aventurine" were re-created in the 1820s for large scale production.

- Famous glass designs such as "millefiori" have been re-created since the 1830s to unknown perfection and diversity.

But the story of the bead industry in the 19th century was determined not only by remarkable progress, but by the contradictory faces of freedom in production and trade. The newly gained freedom gave such strong business-men as the famous Pietro Bigaglia every possible chance to promote the

Four drawn beads of the E. Moretti & f.lli company from Murano, 1920s/30s. These beads represent a very elaborate version of filigree beads. They make use of the classical pattern yet the interpretation is entirely new and very sophisticated as well as labor-intensive.

View of the Canale Grande, Venice, in the 19th century.

Close-up on a sample card of Giorgio Benedetto Barbaria from Venice, 1815 (Technisches Museum, Vienna). G.B. Barbaria donated this sample card to the Habsburg monarch Franz First in 1815. It is the oldest known sample card of Venetian beads which is exactly dated. It supplies a perfect survey on the types of lampworked beads which were made in this period yet these beads are of course the finest possible specimen of each pattern. This part of the sample card includes beads which have long since disappeared from Venetian production lines - such as the faceted ruby-red beads - while, for example, the production of the oblong opalescent beads has been continued throughout the nineteenth century and has even been taken up in Gablonz as well, which means that these beads had been an enormous success on the (African) market. The various design lines of the fancy lampworked beads on this part of the sample card have been made up to the twentieth century, yet they have been varied and eventually simplified.

industry, but also made it possible that pioneering merchants/makers such as Domenico Bussolin would eventually fail and go bankrupt. And many qualified glassmakers, and more specifically lampworkers, who created the tiny vitreous miracles often lived quite a miserable, underpaid existence as a result.

On the initiative of Pietro Bigaglia the "Societa Anonima Fabbriche Unite di Canna, Vetri e Smalti per Conterie" had been founded in 1848. This society was comprised of the most important bead producers of that period including Coen Fratelli, Dalmistro, Errera, and many others. The society had trading posts in Tripoli, Bombay, Calcutta, Alexandria, and Cairo.

Although the bead industry had but one important foreign competitor - the North Bohemian bead industry - it was soon harmed by internal competition. The unification in the "Società" in the mid-19th century had helped to ascertain the bead-monopoly of Murano and Venice. Meanwhile, the demand for glass beads rose higher and higher and the industry expanded, but would

Close-up of the same sample card. This part of the sample card shows again some faceted beads in the colors crystal, red, and blue. This is a standard type of beads which had been made abundantly in Venice in the nineteenth century yet their production had been abandoned and such faceted beads are presently rather associated with the North Bohemian beadindustry.

not reach a similar unity again. For example, in 1874 we can find twenty-three separate producers of bead canes in Murano and Venice, but only two of them were members of the "Società."[1]

In previous periods, the industry had suffered from the excessive unanimity of the bead establishment - now it suffered from the discord of the manufacturers and their readiness to adapt to the ever changing request for beads without coherence. Periods of steep rise were followed by periods of steep decline - for example in 1867, and again in 1874, there was a very high demand for black beads. A hundred years ago such a sudden rise could not be met and prices rose. Now this demand produced an equally high rise in production, followed by a dramatic drop in price when the demand for the black beads slackened. Thus, in 1880 the makers of "macà" - these small black beads - could reach only a third of the price they had been able to ask for in 1874.[2]

Since 1863, Domenico Bussolin had been fighting a second battle in favor of "his" industry - this time against the "pregiudizievole concorrenza"; the highly destructive competition within the industry. In 1876 he hoped to have achieved his goal when the bead manufacturers finally united, only to separate again five months later![3]

Twenty-one years later - in 1898 - seventeen manufacturers joined forces in the "Società Veneziana per la Industria delle Conterie." It became an international company by adding a French and a North Bohemian factory to the group. Thus the society became a presence on their most important fashionable market - France - and had direct access to its most important competitors - the Gablonz industry. After the First World War, the company included further branches of the glass industry and became the "Società Veneziana Conterie e Cristallerie."

Competition from Asian bead industries had been felt since the early 20th century, but did not yet threaten the supremacy of the Venetian and the Gablonz industries. After the Second World War, European glass bead industries lost an important market share of blown beads and drawn beads to Japanese industries, and in recent years Chinese and Indian beadmakers have been gaining an important market share of lampworked beads - most of them being made in the Venetian or Bohemian manner. The end of the "Società" in 1992 was a clear sign of the major changes in this industry. The making of

A book cover which is decorated with yellow beads, Venice, nineteenth century (Glass Museum Murano). This specific variety of beads had been introduced in 1866 by the beadmaker Giovanni Giacomuzzi. They were named "giallo d'oro" (=golden yellow) and were meant to provide really gold-colored beads for precious beadwork.

drawn beads - which were once named "Venetian beads" throughout the world - has been irreversibly passed on to foreign industries, but local makers continue to produce the world's finest and largest selection in fancy lampworked beads.

[1] La Voce di Murano, 15.6.1874:41
[2] La Voce di Murano, 15.5.1874:33 + 15.1.1880:2
[3] La Voce di Murano, 30.10.1877:92

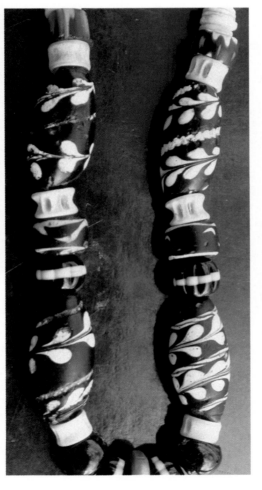

A necklace including four elaborate but partly damaged lampworked beads from Murano/Venice, possibly nineteenth century. These beads represent a standard yet very elaborate interpretation of one pattern which was already included in the Barbaria sample card. Many of those designs of the 1815s sample card survived until the twentieth century yet they found through the long period a great many interpretations. Some are very carefully done and some are visibly done under the pressure to save time as the lampworkers were not paid by the hour but accordding to their output in beads. This necklace was bought in Senegal about fifteen years ago. Such necklaces were made for tourists and they were composed from old and modern beads.

A sample card with elaborate lampworked beads from Murano/Venice, nineteenth century (Glass Museum, Murano). These beads are of the same high quality as the beads on the Barbaria sample card. They have a very elaborate pattern which is built up from (aventurine and) twisted bicolored canes which encircle the bead core. The beads are additionally covered with crystal and the blue-and-white beads on the bottom are even further enhanced with lampworked decorations.

A list of the Italian bead manufacturers/merchants in 1888 from a French directory. Most of them are from Venice. Yet we should keep in mind that the beads were not made by those manufacturers but by thousands of unknown cottage workers in Murano and Venice - most of them being women!

**Italie**

Amonetti, Graziati & Cia, Murano (Venezia).
Angeli (Giuseppe), fabrique d'émaux, rocailles, perles de verre et de coco, Murano presso Venezia.
Arvotti (Serafina), v. Condotti, 4, Roma.
*Barbon (L.) & Cia, alla Maddalena, 2351, Venezia. (V. l'ann. ci-dessous).
Barbon (Isodoro), Castello, Venezia.
Bartolini Torette, v. Frattina, 67 e 68, Roma.
Becher (Federico), Venezia.

*Bonlini & Arbib, Venezia. (Voir l'annonce page 194).
Bordi (Antonio), v. dell'Orso, 83, Roma
Borini, Borri & Cia, S. Salvatore, 5283, Venezia.
*Brinis (Emilio), S. Geremia, 1045, Venezia. (Voir l'ann. page 194).
Ceresa (Agostino), S. Leonardo, 1353, Venezia.
Ceresa (Giac. & Pac.), S. Giobbe, 549, Venezia.
Ceresa (cav. Pacifico fu Luigi), Venezia.
Coen (Marco). Venezia.
Coen (S. S.), Venezia.
Dal Medido (Emilio) & Cia, S. Marco, 218, Venezia.
*Dalmistro e Visentini, Venezia. (Voir l'annonce ci-dessous).
Dona (Giuseppe) & Cia, 11, Murano (Venezia).
Fabbrica Veneziana di perle (Società anonima), S. Simeone, Fondamenta, 561, Venezia.
Flantini (Filippo fu Carlo), Venezia.
Fohr (Leon), Calle della Testa, 6123, Venezia.

Giacommazzi (Ant. fu Ang.), S. Marco, 57, Venezia.
Giove (Pietro Antonio), S. Marziale fond. della Miser., 2339, Venezia.
Girardini (Andrea), S. Marco, 114, Venezia.
Greil (Franc.), S. Ermagora Venezia.
Lacchini (A.), piazza di Spagna, 69, Roma.
Marchi (Teresa), Procurati, 141, Venezia.
Mazzoli (Enrichetta), V. S. Andrea delle Fratte, 7a, Roma.
Pozzi (Vittorio), via della Vite, 51, Roma.
Rey (A.), via Babuino, 121, Roma.
Scandiani (Carlo Samuele fu Marco), Venezia.
Società Unione Industriale Veneziana Montebelluna (Treviso).
Stifoni, Coen & Cia, S. Gerdamo, 3023, Venezia.
*Weberbeck e Cia, Venezia. (Voir l'annonce ci-dessous).
Zecchin (Demetrio & Alessio), Murano (Venezia).

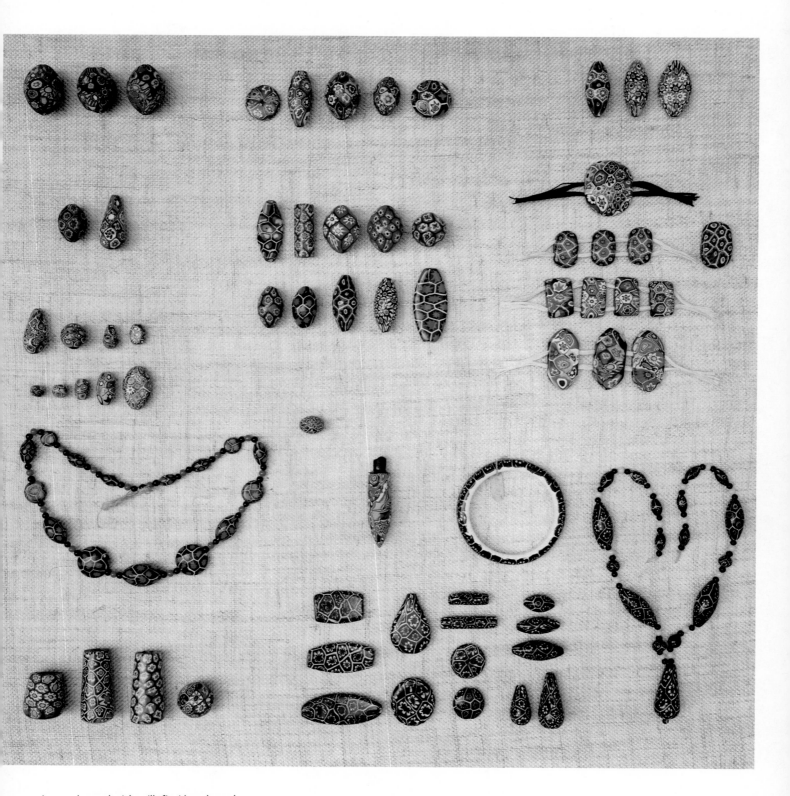

A sample card with millefiori beads and bangles from the E. Moretti & f.lli company in Murano, 1920s. (Courtesy of E. Moretti & f.lli) These millefiori beads reckon among the finest such beads ever made. They excel other such beads because of their elaborate design and their perfect finish. The three necklaces are strung in the typical pattern of the period.

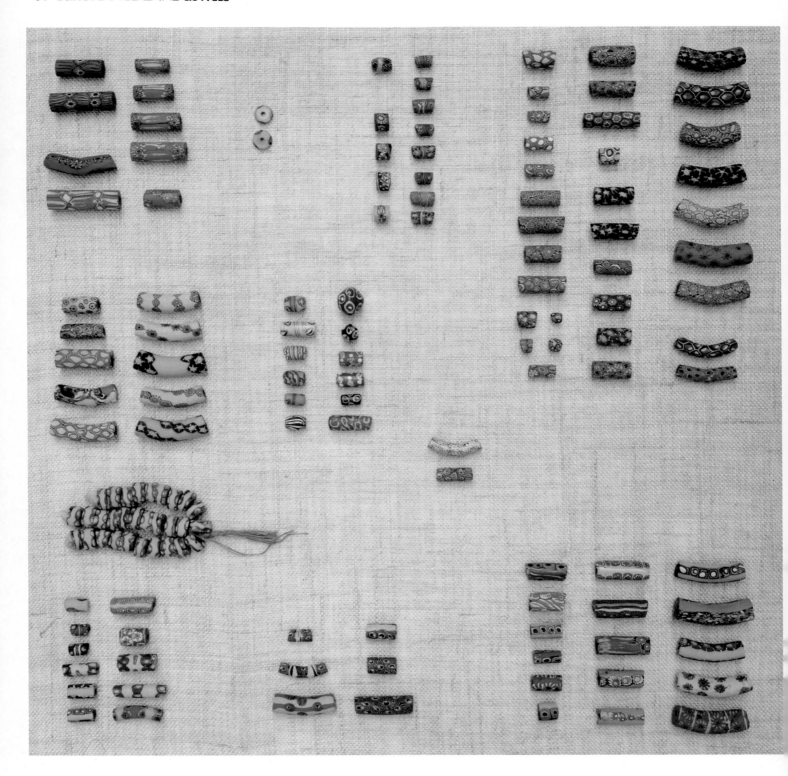

A sample card with millefiori beads, E. Moretti &f.lli, Murano, 1920s and later (Courtesy of E. Moretti & f.lli). These beads were meant for the African trade. Most beads have the typical cylindrical shape which corresponded apparently in some African regions to the traditional bead shape. The design of most beads is very elaborate while many millefiori beads which appear on the African market are less carefully designed showing just a haphazard mixture of multicolored cane segments.

A necklace which had been composed at an unknown period in England of various nineteenth century elements including fine lampworked and gilded beads from Murano/Venice and some small blown "pearls" from Gablonz. The necklace includes a gilded blown bead of the type which is also shown on page 59 (see "The Tyrolian Connection") and some well designed yet fragile gilded beads with blue dots. The making of the gilded beads with the white trailings had been time-consuming as they are covered with an uncommon abundance of trailings.

Five advertisements of Venetian bead manufacturers in 1888 from a French directory.

A gold pendant including an aventurine bead. The bead was made by E. Moretti & f.lli, Murano, 1930s. It represents a typical variety of Moretti beads: it is a drawn bead which is cut from a cane which had been drawn from four separate canes. The four sections are still visible.

Strands of lampworked beads from Murano, first half of the twentieth century. Some among the beads correspond to the beads on the Moretti sample card.

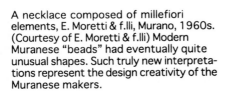

Close-up on a similar necklace of the E.Moretti & f.lli company from Murano, 1960s.

A necklace composed of millefiori elements, E. Moretti & f.lli, Murano, 1960s. (Courtesy of E. Moretti & f.lli) Modern Muranese "beads" had eventually quite unusual shapes. Such truly new interpretations represent the design creativity of the Muranese makers.

A lampworking lady at the E.Moretti & f.lli company from Murano, 1994. She just starts to wind a bead which will include aventurine. Shiny slices of this glass are visible in front of her. The core of the bead is formed with the thick glass cane which she holds in her right hand.

A handfull of millefiori segments. For making millefiori beads the lampworkers will pick up such elements and marver them into a bead core.

Three necklaces including fancy lampworked beads, E. Moretti & f.lli, Murano, 1960s/70s. These beads represent again the innovative strength of the Muranese makers. The beads are made according to century-old patterns yet the interpretation of the themes "stone-bead," "foil-bead," and "trailed bead" is entirely new.

A necklace with lampworked beads from the E. Moretti & f.lli company in Murano, 1994. The beads had been designed by Luciano Moretti. The earpendants were made in a small Muranese workshop by a craftsman whose fiancé had been working with the Morettis. The century-old competition and spying out among the local makers will never cease!

Vases in a Muranese shop, 1994.

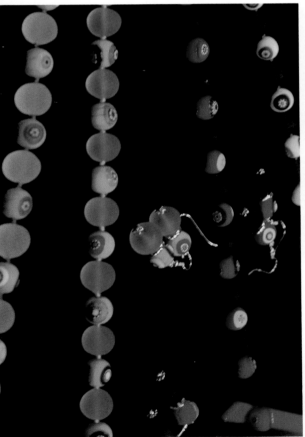

Four blown beads from Murano, 1993. The bead design corresponds exactly to the design of the vases on the previous picture. It is a very old and elaborate design line.

Bottles and beads in Murano, 1994. The design is standard and yet they are eye-catching when seen in such abundance.

A showcase in Venice, 1994, presenting a
fine range of modern lampworked beads.

A modern head bead made by glass artist
Vittorio Costantini from Venice, 1990. The
head-bead-design had been taken up
again on larger scale on the occasion of
the exhibition "I Fenici" (=The Phoenicians)
in 1988.

A showcase in Murano, 1994, with
lampworked items.

## The Dutch and Beads for Africa

The European region which now comprises modern Belgium and the Netherlands became the focal point of trade in Europe towards the end of the Middle Ages. Even most severe political disturbances - the region had belonged to Burgundy since 1363, it became part of the Spanish side of the Habsburg Empire in 1477, the fight for independence of the Dutch began in 1559, and in 1648 the Netherlands gained their independence - did not interrupt the continuous rise of the region, as it was ideally situated for becoming the European doorway to the new world; comprising Africa as well the two Americas, and the European seaway to Asia. The trading triangle between Bruges, Antwerp, and Amsterdam replaced the supremacy of the North Italian city-states, which had been strong as long as the Mediterranean had been important.

Bruges was the most important city among the three during Hanse supremacy in the north. It was connected by a regular shipping line to Spain

A Khoi Khoi women in the 17th century. The Dutch settlers and traders of the 17th century described the elaborate beadwork upon their skin dresses. It was originally done with bronze beads which were later supplanted by Indian glass beads.

Various small striped beads (diameters 3-4 mm), 19th century, uncertain origins. In the background are visible cane segments and beads from Amsterdam, circa 1610. Striped beads were the sucess on the African market - and they were offered in almost unlimited variations from every European bead industry. The beads in the picture are not so common varieties: the bead with the apparently red core is three-layered blue-red-white with ten blue stripes. The two black beads have four times three white stripes and three white and red stripes. The remaining six beads are two-layered blue-white and have each four stripes of different colors.

and Portugal. In the Middle Ages, whoever wanted to buy commodities from Southern Europe and Africa automatically went to Flanders - and in Spain and Portugal, whoever wanted to get fine glass, for example, also went to Flanders.

Around 1500, the sheltered bay which had made Bruges the richest city filled up with sand, and the ships turned towards nearby Antwerp. Around the mid-16th century, Antwerp had become Europe's most important staple, with 500 Dutch merchants and a colony of foreign merchants comprising over 1000 people. The tolerant city became the harbor for Jews from Portugal fleeing Christian fanaticism on the Iberian peninsula: The Teixeira traded in spices and sugar, the Ximenes in precious stones, and the Nunes reckoned among the most appreciated doctors in Antwerp. It was a member of the Ximenes clan from this cosmopolitan city who provided us with important news about European bead production and European bead trade to Africa shortly after 1600. The chemist Emanuele Ximenes corresponded with Antonio Neri in the early 17th century, who would publish his glassmaking manual "De Arte Vetraria" a few years later and was just perfecting his glassmaking skills and knowledge in Florentine and Pisane glassworks. During this time period, Antwerp had to cede its leading role as a trading center to Amsterdam. The "golden century" of Antwerp had come to an end after the Dutch began their fight for freedom. In 1572 they barred the waterway to Antwerp. Amsterdam was to become the leading port - and the 17th century became the "golden century" of Amsterdam. Glass bead production and trade was apparently begun in Antwerp around 1575, yet only twenty-five years later, Ximenes had to travel from Antwerp to Amsterdam to get adequate information about Dutch bead production and bead trade. Amsterdam had become the focus of the European bead trade to the Americas, Africa, and India. Beads were brought from every European bead industry to Amsterdam, from where they were traded into the world.

The first Dutch bead factory is said to have been opened in 1597 in Middelburg. Glassmaking had been started here in 1581 at the entrance towards the Schelde, the waterway to Antwerp. This was a further stroke of the Dutch against the older glass industry of Antwerp - and an indirect attack against the Spanish Habsburgers. Glass production in Amsterdam was apparently begun in 1597.[1] Italian glassmakers had been here even before this period. In 1601 the important glassworks of Jan Hendriksz Soop, which continued work at least until 1623, was opened.[2] An important production line of his factory was beadmaking. Beads were mainly made in winter, while summer was reserved to the production of beakers and other drinking glasses.[3] His products were apparently of great importance for local economy as he succeeded in obtaining a privilege for his production lines. The fact that he employed eighty glassmaking families[4] allows us to conclude that his bead production was quite important. In any case, it was important enough to be shipped not only (via Lisbon) to the Americas and the West Coast of Africa, but also in the same way as Bavarian and Bohemian beads - via Venice - to the Levantine destinations and specifically to Egypt. Such mingling with "their" traditional bead trade routes was considered a severe threat to the local bead industry by Venetian authorities, and in the 18th century it was strictly forbidden to trade foreign beads via Venice.

A necklace with small striped beads from Nagaland/India, nineteenth/twentieth century. The necklace is composed of many different types of striped beads. The great difference in the texture of the beads indicates either different periods or different provenances.

Blue beads, possibly Dutch, uncertain period (Thomas Morbe, Frankfurt). Such large blue beads are mostly attributed to Dutch origin, yet they could have been made in various bead industries north of the Alps.

Four wound beads of various origins, 19th/20th century. Such large monochrome beads were apparently much appreciated in certain areas of Africa and thus they were made in almost every important beadmaking industry, yet it has become customary to attribute them to a Dutch origin. The beads had been oval. They have been cut at the ends, possibly in Africa.

Red beads from Bohemia, 20th century (Thomas Morbe, Frankfurt). This type of bead is often attributed to Dutch origin yet these were made in Bohemia.

The drawn beads which have been excavated in Amsterdam and are attributable to the early 17th century indicate that even the apparently monochrome beads were, in fact, overlay beads. We can learn from the Ximenes-Neri correspondence - where they discuss the varying quality of the coreglass - that such overlay was a standard technique for Dutch beads as well as for Pisane beads.[5] We know that the "Nueva Cadiz" beads which are attributed to the mid-16th - mid-17th century have generally an important core in a different (less attractive) color than the outer layer, and old Rosetta beads also often had an important "colorless" core. Several valuable reasons accounted for this way of combining the compound canes:

- The important use of "colorless," or eventually white, glass helped to considerably reduce the amount of fine colored glass. The two colors which dominate in those early beads - blue and red - gave much technological troubles to the glassmakers and thus were expensive.

- The white layers underneath the red or blue outer layers gave more brilliance to those two colors.

- The types of glass chosen for the (major part of) the core might have been specifically suitable for drawing long canes with an adequate hole - as the brilliantly colored glass of the outer layers was quite often rich in lead and thus rather soft.

The major part of the beads which were shipped from Amsterdam into the world apparently came from Nuremberg and Venice - yet Ximenes reported in 1603 that two manufacturers/merchants from Amsterdam were involved in the bead trade and ran four furnaces for making beads without interruption.[6] Ximenes' letters reveal a lot about the promptness with which Dutch beadmakers tried to respond to African demand for certain bead designs. We also learn from him that the Pisane workshops apparently produced a large selection of fine beads. He was even tempted to enter the bead trade with beads from Pisa, yet desisted from it when he realized how difficult it was to respond to the very specified demand of the Africans.[7] Upon precise African request, striped beads seem to have been an overwhelming success on the West African coast in this early 17th century. We learn this from Ximenes and it is also confirmed by beads which have been found in Amsterdam, as the striped beads clearly prevail among them. In 1603 Ximenes reported that only a single bead design was requested in West Africa - light blue beads with up to three white stripes.[8]

In the 17th century Dutch makers produced drawn beads, blown beads, and wound beads. Since the beads for Africa were designed according to African wishes, many Dutch beads necessarily looked similar to Venetian beads, yet this fact doesn't answer the question of who had been the first one to offer those beads. It is generally assumed that the Dutch beadmakers imitated Venetian bead design. Blown glass "in the Venetian manner" was abundantly made in German and Dutch glassworks yet there is no conclusive evidence that the same happened in the matter of bead design. I would rather presume that the Dutch preceded the Venetians at least in the making of those striped beads - as the Dutch were more deeply and directly involved in the West African bead trade than any other European country, including Venice. Ximenes' letter wouldn't make sense if those lightblue beads with white stripes were already a customary bead design from Venice in 1603, and it would have been a daring task if the Dutch beadmakers - who, according to the Amsterdam bead finds, largely concentrated on the striped beads - had attempted to enter the bead market with an already wellestablished design of an experienced beadmaking industry. It makes more sense to assume that the Dutch were the first to respond to this new demand from Africa. As striped beads apparently became the most successful beads on the African market, at least during the 17th century, the experienced

Muranese/Venetians took up this design line as well, and eventually outdid the Dutch "newcomers" during the 17th century. The leading role of the striped beads in African trade of the 17th century is confirmed by the fact that the drawing of such striped canes is recorded as the basic task for becoming cane master in Murano in 1667.[9]

Another variety of glass beads which has remained highly appreciated among the Yoruba apparently originated in the early years of the 17th century and was also possibly made first by Dutch (or the Bavarian) beadmakers: in his letters of 1603 Ximenes repeatedly reported the urgent request of Africans from the Guinean Coast for a type of glass beads which should closely resemble a rare natural stone, for which they would pay their weight in gold.[10] Although the description of Ximenes is slightly confusing, it can be deduced that the beads should be semi-transparent and have a bluish tint when looked upon and a yellowish tint when looked across. These indications point to an imitation of either moonstone - a feldspar variety - or a similarly looking agate variety - both stones which occur in Africa. Only a single type of glass corresponds to this demand - the opalescent glass. This pressing demand from Africa caused hectic activity in Amsterdam as well as in Pisa. The first samples of glass were exchanged between Neri and Ximenes, but these first attempts were apparently not satisfactory. The Africans were also not satisfied with the first such beads they got from the Dutch, as they had apparently tried to achieve the desired color with blown and lined beads. Yet plenty of opalescent beads are found among the bead finds from Amsterdam which are attributed to a few years later, 1610. And the mysterious "Schiller" beads from Bavaria (see pages 31-32) might equally be such opalescent beads - specifically as the bead-related contact between Nuremberg and Amsterdam was very close. The first written record about similar glass from Murano - the "girasole" - is dated 1693.[1] The fact that those beads became an important production line in Murano is recorded in 1766, when the Muranese got their privilege for the production of certain bead types confirmed: "Girasole" beads were explicitly mentioned on this occasion.[12]

In a letter written to the Amsterdam authorities, Soop insisted on having brought beadmaking to Amsterdam.[13] This statement is not too reliable as it was made to obtain certain privileges - yet it would make sense economically that the Dutch only truly became involved in beadmaking when

Opalescent beads, uncertain origin and period. (Thomas Morbe, Frankfurt) Such opalescent beads had most likely been created for the first time upon African request in the early 17th century. They were highly appreciated and in Yoruba society have remained reserved for the use of the priests until modern times. It is recorded that such beads were made in Bavaria, Bohemia, Murano, and in the Netherlands.

Opalescent beads attributed to Dutch origin, uncertain period. (Thomas Morbe, Frankfurt)

Opalescent beads from Gablonz, 20th century (Thomas Morbe, Frankfurt). This beadshape was named "Birnel" (=pear) and was made exclusively for the African trade.

The building of the company Fried Frères in Gablonz. This French company grew from the Bohemian export house Erich Rähm in Wiesenthal near Gablonz. In 1922 they opened their new building directly in Gablonz from where the company traded specifically to the French colonies in North Africa.

they had replaced the Portuguese on the African coast and in India, and had established their pre-colonial trading network. Further bead factories are known from places like Harlem and Rotterdam - but apparently most of the Dutch beadworks did not exist beyond the 17th century. It seems as if Dutch bead production declined as soon as Dutch supremacy around Africa was supplanted by the French and the English. Yet Dutch producers must have continued to offer a specifically Dutch bead design: Heinrich von Minutoli - who was a very reliable chronicler - confirmed in 1824 that most beads which reached Africa via Egypt were indeed beads from Murano/Venice, but a specific type "3/4 blue and 1/4 white" (possibly blue with white stripes?) came from the Netherlands.[14]

[1]Baart, 1986:66
[2]ibid.:66
[3]ibid.:70
[4]ibid.:70
[5]Zecchin I, 1987:172
[6]ibid.:172
[7]ibid.:172
[8]ibid.:172
[9]Zecchin II, 1989:110
[10]Zecchin I, 1987:172/173
[11]Zecchin, 1986:63
[12]Cecchetti, 1874:276
[13]Baart, 1986:66
[14]Minutoli, 1824:365

## France and False Pearls

In the Middle Ages France had a thriving glass industry, producing the finest colored glass for windows, small fashionable items such as false gems and glass inlays for furniture, splendid enamelwork, and at least in Southern France, fine blown glass. In early periods, France had neither an economic nor a fashionable reason to become deeply involved in beadmaking - except for artificial pearls - and this involvement apparently began based on the fancy lampworking "in the Venetian manner."

French interest in such glass began in the mid-16th century. French royalties took a fancy in attracting Italian glassmakers to France for making similar glass, as it had become a real craze among the upper classes in France. Those Italians came from various glassmaking regions, but mostly from Altare in the Duchy of Montferrat. One of these was a certain Teseo Mutio, who came from Bologna, and who obtained certain privileges for making "Venetian" glass from Henry the Second, including canes from opaque glass, in the Royal glassworks at Saint-Germain-en-Laye near Paris during the second half of the 16th century.[1] It seems he was not very successful,[2] and if he ever made canes they were primarily used for making the fancy lampworked items which became very fashionable in France. Such lampwork was begun in France in the last third of the 16th century, and the region of Nevers in particular became famous for making fancy figurines and similar items.

At Rouen in Normandy in the late 16th century there were glass beadmakers which had acquired corporate status in 1593 and which lampworked beads and buttons and further small objects. It is said that they got the necessary canes from local glassworks.[3] They might have done wound lampworked beads - as buttons were generally done in this technique - but by the beginning of the 17th century, the French had already become so

Lampworking in France in the eighteenth century. This illustration is included in the French translation of J. Kunkel's "Ars Vitraria" or "Glasmacherkunst" (see page 111) which had been published in 1752 in Paris. Two men and a woman are assembled around a working table with a huge vent underneath for supplying the flames of their tallow lamps with sufficient air. The long glass canes which they hold in their hands are thus reheated until they turn malleable. The softened glass is shaped into fancy items with the help of the kind of pincers which they hold in their other hand —a tool which is also depicted below. The three lampworkers do not make beads. This would have required different tools.

Strands of gold-lined bugles from France, early twentieth century. Even such relatively large beads were used for beadwork upon textiles. France was a leading producer of dresses with elaborate beadwork decorations.

Advertisement of the company Klaar in a French directory of 1888. The Bohemian beadmakers which were internationally represented by such important export houses as the company Klaar had very close links with the French market - often even with affiliates in Paris.

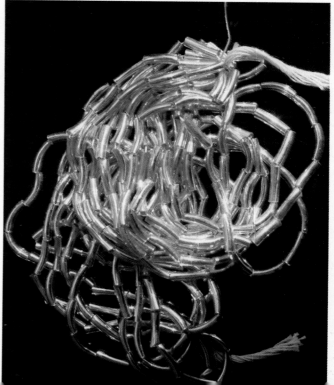

**FRANCE**

**Paris**

Audy (Vve L.), r. Montmorency, 40.
Mandailles, r. de Bagnolet, 73.
Ruteau (L. & H.) frères, r. Chapon, 31.

**Calvados**

Deléan, à Argences.

**Cher**

Auclerc (Ant.), Jouet-s.-l'Aubois.
Dutet (C.), perles blanches, à St-Germain-sur-l'Aubois.

**Haute-Loire**

Faurry, à Langeac.
Martin-Dieudonnat (V•),à Langeac.
Parrier, à Langeac.

**Loiret**

Bapterosses (T.), à Briare.

**Sarthe**

Gervais & Cⁱᵉ, à Saint-Mars-de-Locquenay.

**Seine-et-Oise**

Brunet, à Herblay.
Garry, à Herblay.
Lhuillier, à Boisemont.
Samson, à Cormeilles-en-Parisis.

List of the French suppliers of glass beads and glass pearls in 1888. The number of French manufacturers/merchants can't compare with the Italian and Bohemian number of the same period.

A necklace including flat lampworked beads, Rousselet company, Paris, 1920s/30s. The beads are coral-colored. The elaborate metal elements between the beads include tiny glass pearls and faceted glass stones.

involved with lamp-blowing that I would suspect the makers in Rouen concentrated on blowing as well. Henry the Fourth continued to increase the importance of Rouen as a glassmaking center in the French north by attracting further experienced glassmakers to the town, in 1598 two from the Duchy of Mantua and in 1605 one from Southern France. We can learn from 1613 records that the Provençal lamp-worked as well, yet the records don't tell whether he made beads.[4]

As false pearls had become a fashionable craze throughout Europe since the second half of the 16th century, blown glass pearls also began to be made around the same time in many European countries - yet their production on a large scale was only started in the 17th century, in other countries as well as in France. Besides beads, early French lamp-blowers made technical utensils and artificial eyes, two production lines which remained important for them until the 20th century. As the "pearls" were of such great importance for the European market, everybody tried to improve their making. In France, two lampworkers from Nevers - Ja(c)quin and Breton - perfected their lining in 1686.[5] 17th century French "pearl" production was a proper bead industry, producing for export and fully conquering the English market but not continental markets, where too many similar industries competed with the French. They held a near-monopoly on the English market until the late 18th century.[6]

Information about the eventual making of small drawn beads in the 17th century comes from Haudicquer de Blancourt, who is not a very reliable chronicler. For example, in 1697 he published his "Art de la Verrerie," professed to be an original text, which Georges Bontemps recognized as "a compilation of the recipes he could collect in Neri and from his contemporaries."[7] Documents of the 18th century refer to "petits grains superfains"[8], a designation which possibly refers to French-made small drawn beads, yet it is also recorded from this century that French enamelers imported small Bohemian beads or at least the bead glass rich in lead to crush them/it and to use the crushed glass for enamelwork.[9]

Beaded flowers from Bohemia, late nineteenth/early twentieth century. Since at least the nineteenth century, France had a thriving industry for "couronnes mortuaires," i.e. grave ornaments assembled from such beaded flowers.

Three necklaces including coral-colored glass beads and Galalith beads, possibly Rousselet, Paris, 1930s/50s.

Close-up on the necklaces of the previous picture. The "coral" beads are of such exceptional quality that one is easily mistaken about the material yet those glass beads are heavier than coral beads would be.

A necklace with sophisticated glass beads, created by the glass artist René Lalique from Paris, circa 1908-1909 (Courtesy Schmuckmuseum Pforzheim, photograph by Günter Meyer). Ten glass scarabs are mounted in gold and connected to ten rectangular glass elements.

Two necklaces of the company Rousselet from Paris, 1920s/30s. The large beads are flat with a slightly irregular surface. The necklaces also include artificial pearls.

The French "pearl" industry grew considerably in the last third of the 18th century. Nevers remained the most important region for such lamp-work, but industries in Rouen were also enlarged. In addition, pearlmaking became concentrated around Paris - as it had a tendency to develop close to fashionable capitals - and even Marseille, far in the south, became a pearlmaking center.[10] According to the records of Giorgio Barbaria from Murano in 1776, the French imported Muranese canes on a large scale for making their artificial pearls, pretending to use them for making technical utensils such as barometers,[11] while Barrelet reports that the necessary "girasole" was produced in French factories.[12] Both reports are probably true, as the demand for artificial pearls was high enough in the fashionable world that "pearl"making was based on every possible supply of canes. French pearl production declined during the 19th century and ceded its market shares to its German and Bohemian competitors. The remnants of this industry concentrated around Paris.[13]

At about the same time, France entered the bead market with a new production line, the first entirely machine-made beads, named Porcelain beads; because of their appearance, or Bapterosses beads; after the manufacturer who launched them onto the European market. Jean Felix Bapterosses, from Briare on the river Loire, had introduced those beads, which were made based on a technique that had been developed around 1840 by the Prosser brothers in England for making buttons.

Around 1900, small "Rocailles" started to be produced in France on larger scale: the Venetian "Società" had settled in 1898 in France by buying a French company. The French "Société" had factories in Paris and in Bron, close to Lyon. In addition, the "Compagnie Française pour l'industrie de la perle" was founded in 1900 with factories in Chauny(Aisne) and in Saint-Quentin.[14]

In the early 20th century glass-artist René Lalique began to make exceptional Art Nouveau glass beads, and in 1922, the bead manufacturer Pierre Rousselet began making beads in Paris. His most important work consisted of very fashionable beads from Galalith and high quality lampworked beads.

[1]Barrelet, 1953:65
[2]Gerspach, 1885:198
[3]ibid.:233/234
[4]ibid.:234
[5]Barrelet, 1953:92
[6]Savi alla Mercanzia, Diversorum, busta 385,58 (State Archives of Venice)
[7]Bontemps, 1868:8
[8]Barrelet, 1953:118
[9]Pazaurek, 1911:10
[10]Barrelet, 1953:118
[11]Gasparetto, 1958:192
[12]Barrelet, 1953:119
[13]Péligot, 1877:462
[14]Exposition Internationale Urbaine de Lyon, 1914, rapport générale, no date:441

## Russian "Bisser" and "Russian" Beads

Russia knew two short but splendid bead production periods. Glassmaking was well established in the Kiev Rus (now Ukraine) between the 11th - 13th century. This production included the making of drawn beads and bangles in many colors.

The bead-related history of modern times began with the import of Bohemian beads in the 18th century and the adoption of the Bohemian term for drawn beads. The Russian term for small standard drawn beads generally meant for beadwork, is "Bisser" (German transcription). This Russian term is derived from the old German term, "Bissel," for the small drawn beads. The term had possibly been introduced in Russia in the mid-18th century when the existing glass and bead trading links between Bohemia and St. Petersburg became very intensive and close - equalling in importance the Bohemian trading contacts with Amsterdam, Lisbon, and Cadiz.[1]

Russian bead production was taken up shortly afterwards. In 1752/53, the Russian scientist Michael Lomonosov (1711-1765), who had conducted intensive research on colored glass, founded his own factory at Ust'Ruditsa near St. Petersburg. There he made mosaic tesserae, beads, and bugles. The decision to take up bead production was possibly a result of a real craze for bead and bugle embroidery in Russia at this time. This enthusiasm for beadwork produced absolutely outstanding pieces, among them the beaded panels which are found in the "bugle room" of the Chinese Palace in Oranienbaum near St. Petersburg. After Lomonosov's death in 1765, the factory only survived until 1768, and the high-quality Russian bead industry thus ended after only fifteen years.

Russian beadwork was again made from Bohemian and Venetian beads - with a close link to the Bohemian industries. Thus the Russian fur trade of the 19th century in Russian America (Alaska) relied very much on Bohemian "Sprengperlen" as well as on Thuringian "Schmelzperlen" - beads of the same appearance as the Bohemian ones yet generally cut from thinner tubes. These were rather large drawn beads which were just cut from the cane and not given any further finishing except that they were cut on the ends - a treatment which gave them the appearance of being slightly faceted. The predominance of such beads in the Russian trade led to the assumption that these beads were of Russian make and thus they were named "Russian" beads.

[1]Schebek, 1969:63,126,238,254

Close-up on a beaded panel in the "bugle" room of the Chinese Palace, Oranienbaum/St. Peterburg, 1760s. The beadwork is mainly composed from "Atlas" glass bugles.

Close-up on a mosaic made with Lomonosov tesserae, St. Petersburg, eighteenth century (Hermitage, St. Petersburg).

An inkbottle enclosed with beadwork, Russia, 1797. The cock is a dominant folk art motif in Russia.

A beaded bag from Russia, modern. Such modern beadwork is frequently based on traditional folk art motifs and uses also the traditional color combinations.

The Russian lady which made the necklace and the earpendants and sold them in the streets of St. Petersburg to the foreign tourists.

An icon mounting with beads and artificial gems, Russia, nineteenth century.

A necklace and earpendants from St. Petersburg, 1993. The beadwork is arranged upon a saucer from the famous porcelain factory of St. Petersburg showing the same colors and motifs which are found in other Russian crafts and in the beadwork as well.

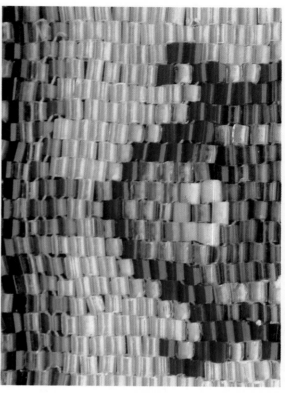

"Russian" beads from Gablonz or Thuringia, late nineteenth century.

Glass birds made by glass artist V. Muratov, Gus-Khrustalny glassworks, Russia, modern. Here we find again the cock motif which dominates so very much in Russian folk art.

A bell handle from Germany, late nineteenth century, composed from simple "Sprengperlen" as those drawn beads were named.

A modern Russian beadwork necklace. Beadworking is again taken up in modern Russia and many young artists create fanciful beaded jewelry.

"Russian" beads from Gablonz or Thuringia, late nineteenth century. The beads are arranged upon a background showing parts of a Russian costume including plenty of such beads.

A candle holder from Thuringia, nineteenth/twentieth century. Such larger items were blown from relatively thick glass. They were silver-lined in the same way as the blown beads or the Christmas decorations and they were mostly enhanced by paintings on the outside.

## *Blueberries and Mirror Beads - Beadmaking in the Thuringian Forest*

Thuringian glassmaking began in the Middle Ages with strong familial links to the famous glassmaking regions further west. Recent research has revealed such an important involvement of Thuringian merchants in the long distance trade between the Rhineland and Byzantium since the 6th/7th century AD,[1] that one might suspect Thuringian bead production to have already existed in this early period.

"Modern" Thuringian glassmaking was initiated during the 16th century by waves of immigrants. In the early 16th century, Thuringian glassmaking was strongly reinforced by immigrants from the west and Frankonia. The glassmakers of this period are known to have produced window glass, as well as high quality blown glass suitable for enameling and engraving. Thuringian glass engravers had a European-wide reputation.[2] Other immigrants arrived in the second half of the 16th century - among them Hans Greiner and Christoph Müller. They founded the first glassworks in Lauscha in 1597. Glassmaking in and around Lauscha was originally based on the production of drinking glasses and small bottles, but Lauscha was to become the Thuringian center for bead and marblemaking, the production of fancy lampwork including toys, Christmas decorations, and artificial eyes in the mid-18th century. Thuringian lampwork spread into the northwesterly parts of the Thuringian Forest in the early 19th century as well, but in this region the industry concentrated on producing technical glass instead.

The Thuringian bead industry produced above all three basic types of beads:

- Drawn beads which were cut from rather thin tubes, and which got no further treatment except of eventual lining. They were named "Schmelzperlen."

- Blown beads in a tremendous range of fancy shapes. Those blown beads were mainly lined either with "essence d'orient" (a solution created from fish scales which gave it a pearly sheen) and transformed into artificial pearls, or lined with a metallic solution to produce the "Spiegelperlen" (=mirror beads).

- Massive beads which in modern times were cut mainly from filigree canes. Identical marbles were produced as well.

The Thuringian beads were exported mainly to the Netherlands up to the mid-19th century, from where they were sent into the world.[3]

The making of the blown beads was exclusively a cottage industry, generally involving the entire family. In 1872, Lauscha counted fifty such beadmaking families.[4] In peak periods, every lampworking family was involved in beadmaking and when the demand for blown beads slackened, a major part turned back once again to the other production lines.

One of the founding dynasties of the Lauscha glass industry - the Greiner - was also very involved in the various fields of beadmaking. Ferdinand Friedrich Greiner (1808-1885) concentrated on blown beads.[5] In 1849 Elias Greiner perfected the making of glass marbles and the corresponding beads with his "marble scissors."[6] Originally, these marbles and beads were not made in the now customary version with colorful filigree twists, but from "stone" glass imitating agate, lapis, topaz, and other semiprecious stones just as early marbles were made in the German stone industries. As the demand for blown beads rose steeply around the mid-19th century, Elias Greiner extended his production to include glass canes, glass tubes, and blown beads.

The Thuringian lampworkers were extremely experienced in other branches of lampworking as well - specifically the production of technical glass - and as the demand for such products rose continually, they reduced beadmaking during the second half of the 19th century and turned towards the branches where their skills were unequalled. This included not only technical glass, but fancy lampworking of sophisticated and fragile drinking vessels and similar items as well. The many varieties of beads which had been created in Thuringia were produced in greater amount in the North Bohemian bead industry after the late 19th century.

[1]Claude, 1985: 156
[2]Pazaurek, 1933:325
[3]Deutsche Gewerbezeitung, 1858:130
[4]Hoffmann, 1976:26
[5]Löber, 1926:16
[6]Kühnert, 1973:247

Buttons versus beads: a costume from Northern Germany, late nineteenth century. The costume includes elaborate beadwork on the cap and three rows of large artificial pearls from Thuringia across the chest - yet these delicate ornaments are outdone by the overlarge silver buttons.

The panorama of Lauscha in 1864. Lauscha was but a humble village and yet it supplied in those years the whole world with its blown mirror beads, black beads - named "blueberries" - and artificial pearls.

Christmas decorations from Thuringia, nineteenth/twentieth century. Such silvered decorations were a major production line of the Thuringian cottage workers.

Thuringian lampworkers in 1883. On this picture the lampworkers are assembled in a large well-lit workshop. Generally such work was done in the cottages with the help of the entire family. Those beadmakers worked under incredibly unhealthy conditions as the small rooms in which they lived and worked were almost permanently filled with suffocating fumes.

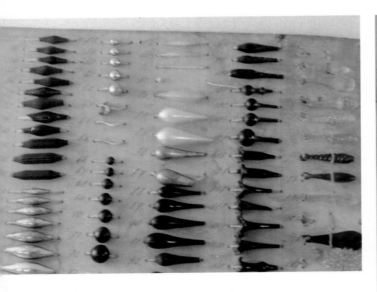

A sample card with blown beads from Lauscha, nineteenth/twentieth century (Glass Museum Lauscha). This card includes mainly black beads and silvered beads and a few massive lampworked beads in the right row. Among the black beads are the famous Thuringian "blueberries" in various sizes. The perfectly round beads which had been created in the 1850s got this name.

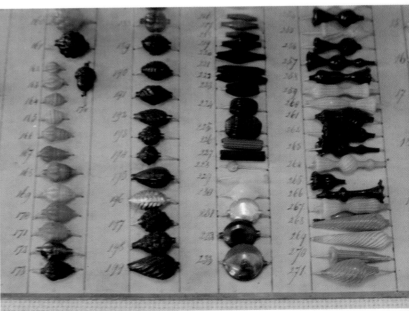

A sample card including blown beads from Lauscha, nineteenth/twentieth century (Glass Museum Lauscha). This card includes beads in many fancy shapes and they are lined with many different colors. The beads in the right row are made from glass canes with aventurine stripes.

Elaborate lamp work from Lauscha, circa 1840 (Glass Museum Lauscha). The figurine and the horse is blown. Thuringian makers mastered such fragile blown lamp work in unequalled perfection.

Three tankards from Thuringia, late nineteenth/early twentieth century. A major part of the Thuringian glass was transformed into canes and tubes for lampworking yet the industry produced also standard blown glass such as those tankards.

Strands of blown beads from Lauscha, early twentieth century. The beads are blown from glass with delicate aventurine stripes. They resemble the beads on the sample card.

Six striped marbles from Thuringia, late nineteenth/early twentieth century. Such marbles were made for the European and the North American market and identical beads were made for Africa.

Bad Ilmenau/Thuringia in 1897. The Thuringian glassmaking villages were highly appreciated holiday ressorts. The many tourists which always took great pleasure in visiting the glassworks and the lamp-workshops gave the glassmakers and lampworkers the chance of an extra income.

A sample card with two rows of blown beads from Lauscha, early twentieth century (Glass Museum Lauscha). One row of beads is silver-lined and the other row is lined with a luminescent color.

A lampworker in Lauscha, 1990.

A necklace with blown beads from
Thuringia, 1920s. The "white" beads are
lined with a luminescent color. Such beads
were a real craze in the 1920s/30s.

## "Paterln" - The Beads From Frankonia/Bavaria

To date, the history of bead production in the Fichtelmountains has
not been sufficiently researched. Glass and bead production began in this
area possibly as early as the 9th century AD.[1]

Folk-lore claims the Venetians as the initiators of the local bead
industry, dating its origin in the late 15th century. Yet these legends are
debatable as the dominant production mode of the Fichtelmountains beads -
furnace winding - suggests a much older origin. Claiming descendance from
Venetian glassmakers was simply a means to improve the reputation of the
local industry in many European glassmaking areas - as "Venetian" was the
key-word for quality and fashionable design in glass (just as Bohemian and
Muranese beads intentionally adopted the label "French" in the 19th and 20th
centuries, and thus sold much better).

However old-fashioned and even primitive furnace-winding might
appear compared to other more sophisticated techniques in beadmaking,
the industry flourished in the Fichtelmountains until the early 20th century.
During this period, production was once again considerably diversified.
Beads were offered in various nuances of forty different basic shades and
many different sizes corresponding to the weight of 150 g/1000 beads up to 10
kg/1000 beads.[2] This industry survived until the 1960s, when the last furnace
was finally closed. However simple the common furnace-wound beads might
appear on the surface, they deserve closer study. At least some of the large
opalescent and white beads, which were highly appreciated in Africa, and
which are generally attributed to other origins, come in fact from the
Fichtelmountains where they were named "Taubeneiperlen" (=dove's egg
beads).[3]

[1]Veh, 1964/65:
[2]Pazaurek, 1911:7
[3]ibid.:7

A necklace with blown filigree beads
made by glass artist Albin Schaedel from
Thuringia, 1990.

Advertisement of the company S. Lindner
from Warmensteinach in 1888.

**Allemagne**

Bettmann & Kupfer, Baireuth.
Bunte (C.), Schönbrunn, b. Wunsiedel (Bayern).
Dost & Blechschmiedt, Warmensteinach, b. Baireuth.
Drassel (J.), Warmensteinach (Bayern)
Glaswaarenfabrik Marienthal, bei Sonneberg (Thüringen).
Greiner & Cᵒ, Bischoffsgrün (Bayern).
Hermann (G.), Warmensteinach, b. Bayreuth.
Hermann (Heinrich), Warmensteinach (Bayern).
Kühnert (G.) & Co, Ernstthal-Lauscha.
Lindenfels (Freih. v.), Atenstadt, bei Erbendorf.
Lindner (Sigm.), Warmensteinach (Bayern). (Voir *Verroterie*).
Pschörer (Chr.), Unterlind, b. Baireuth (Bayern).
Rabenstein, Warmensteinacher-Perlenfabrik, Ober-Warmensteinach.
Risler & Cᵒ, et boutons en porcelaine, Freiburg (Baden).
Scharrer (II.) & Koch, Baireuth.
Schmidt (Max), Baireuth.
Schott & Hermann, Warmensteinach.
Trassl (Michael), Oberwarmensteinach (Bayern).

A list of German bead manufacturers/bead trading companies in 1888. Most of them are from the Fichtelmountains or from places close to those mountains such as Bayreuth.

White beads of uncertain origin and period (Thomas Morbe, Frankfurt). Such large white beads were made in various European bead industries. In the Fichtelmountains - where their production is at least recorded from the early 20th century, they were named "Taubeneiperlen."

Beadmakers in Warmensteinach in the early twentieth century (Photo: Röthel, Warmensteinach).

A basket decorated with Bavarian beads, 1930s. Bavarian beads were frequently used for the decoration of such very common items.

Close-up on a sample card with Bavarian beads, 1930s.

Various Bavarian beads, twentieth century. The beads are lined with paint.

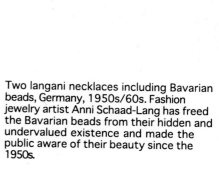

Beaded mats and flowerpot holders which were assembled from locally made beads by cottage workers in and around Warmensteinach, 1930s (Photo: Röthel, Warmensteinach).

Two langani necklaces including Bavarian beads, Germany, 1950s/60s. Fashion jewelry artist Anni Schaad-Lang has freed the Bavarian beads from their hidden and undervalued existence and made the public aware of their beauty since the 1950s.

## North Bohemian Beads

### "Schürer" beads

Since the late 15th century, glassmaking in North Bohemia had been almost exclusively in the hands of three leading dynasties - the Preussler, the Schürer, and the Wander. Their excellent glass was so highly appreciated that one of the families - the Schürer - was advanced to nobility in 1592 by the emperor Rudolf the Second. The Schürer were not only excellent glassmakers, but also versatile businessmen - almost equal, on a smaller scale, to the famous Fugger dynasty from Augsburg.

Because of the close contact the Schürer held with this important trading capital, it may have been from here that they got their inspiration for making glass beads. Yet as North Bohemia had equally excellent trading links to the Ottoman Empire - from where the Muranese most likely received their inspiration for making glass canes - they may have been induced to beadmaking by Arab merchants as well. We don't know when exactly the Schürer began beadmaking, but its production is confirmed from their Krombach glassworks which lit its furnaces in the early 16th century and stopped working before the end of the 17th century. Glass beads in various colors have been excavated on the site.[1] Krombach was situated close to an important trade route which connected North Bohemia to Saxonia and Silesia, and may have influenced the origin of this production line - as vitreous paternoster beads had become a frequent commodity.

Many Schürers spread from Krombach to further glassworks and it is possible that beadmaking spread with them. Yet there exist no written records about this production line; sources refer only to the luxury glass which the Schürer supplied to the Bohemian court. The scarcity of written records regarding the production of the glassworks is rather typical for this region, as those isolated makers lacked any organization comparable to the urban guilds which recorded the activities of the craftsmen in the cities with scrupulous care.

The making of wound beads and buttons in this area is confirmed from at least the 17th century in other glassworks, such as from Witkowitz (1606-1795), as well.[2]

The first written record about bead production comes from the Grünwald glass works near Gablonz - referring to black beads in 1740.[3] The source doesn't tell when this production was started, but the involvement of the versatile Schürer, which had direct contacts to the important Italian glassmaking area Altare,[4] in this production allows for the assumption that beadmaking was never discontinued in this area once they had begun it.

[1]Fischer, 1924:26
[2]Zenkner, 1968:42
[3]Jargstorf, 1993:65
[4]Zenkner, 1968:22

### The Riedels and beadmaking

The 18th century brought a serious crisis to Muranese/Venetian glass and beadmaking, as well as the Bohemian glass industries. North Bohemia was able to overcome this crisis with a completely new structure for the industries. Since about 1700, the old glass dynasties had begun to disappear into other professions - thus escaping the need to conform to new commercial necessities. The closing of the old glasshouses was soon followed by a new

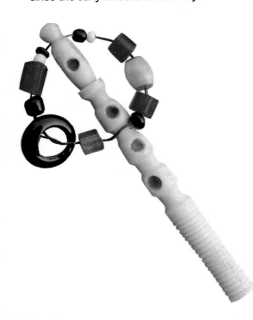

*I. Wappen der Schürer von Waldheim 1592.*

The family crest of the Schürer dynasty. The Schürer had been involved with beadmaking possibly since the 16th century and certainly since the 17th century.

A bobbin including various beads from North Bohemia, nineteenth century. Furnace wound ringlets and drawn beads like the three blue beads and the crystal bead had been made in the Gablonz area since the late eighteenth century. Blown beads had equally been made since the late eighteenth century yet the blown mother-of-pearl beads like the light blue one had most likely only been made since the early nineteenth century.

Blue faceted beads from Gablonz, 19th century (Thomas Morbe, Frankfurt). Such oblong faceted blue beads were apparently a bead variety which was much appreciated in certain area of Africa.

beginning, largely based upon the dominant glass merchants who influenced the structure of production and decided upon the necessary production and design lines. Yet at least around Gablonz, their strength was counterbalanced by a new glassmaking dynasty - the Riedel. The Riedel sprang from a legendary glass merchant and started glassmaking in the 1750s with a single glassworks - eventually dominating glass production in this area with more than a dozen glassworks, some of which had been founded for the sole purpose of making tubes and canes for the local bead industry. The Riedels had an important part in making Gablonz the leading beadmaking area north of the Alps. In the 19th century, the Gablonz bead industry became the only important rival to the Muranese/Venetian bead industry.

The making of drawn beads in the Gablonz area is noted for the first time in the late 18th century in Morchenstern and Neudorf. It has not been ascertained where the necessary tubes and canes came from, or whether this bead production was derived from the nearby Grünwald glassworks. Yet it is also recorded that the Riedel glassworks in Neuwiese (1756-1817) and Christiansthal (1775-1887), and the Unger glassworks in Tiefenbach (1787-1830), sold tubes in 1790 and 1800. Their cane and tube production must have begun earlier, as we know that in the early years of this production, the beads were cut within the glassworks.[1] As there was no technical need to accomplish this in the actual glassworks, beadcutting was soon given to cottage workers. The early beadcutters still lived close to the corresponding glassworks, in the valleys north of Gablonz, but by and by the tedious work moved south through Morchenstern and Labau settling in the Czech villages south of Gablonz in 1870.

The drawn beads of the late 18th and the early 19th century were mostly large beads of the type known to American bead collectors as "Russian" beads. In the very beginning the beads were cut from round tubes. It is recorded from the early 19th century that the canes were molded with six to eight sides, thus giving the beads a basic set of facets - yet presumably the molding began in the 18th century, as the first such beads are recorded from North America in the late 18th century. Yet the possibility remains that those early beads came from the older beadmaking area, the Bavarian/Bohemian Forest. Originally, those "Sprengperlen" were finished by cutting them at the ends with further facets, but the finishing work on them was reduced eventually. Higher productivity was first achieved by simply tumbling them with an abrasive and already by the mid-19th century a major part of them was cut from thinner tubes, receiving no further finishing treatment except for eventual lining. During the second half of the 19th century this production line came more or less to an end, as the beads were replaced by the machine-made "porcelain" beads (see "France and False Pearls"). The production of "porcelain" beads was taken up in Gablonz in the year 1885 by the Redlhammers who produced them successfully until 1945.[2]

From the very beginning of their bead production, the Gablonzers had also produced small beads and bugles which were finished in the same (mechanical) way as the large "Sprengperlen," but apparently the Gablonz beadmakers did not begin to compete with the Muranese bead industry in the matter of small "Rocailles" - which were finished by reheating - until the 1840s. It seems the manufacturer Josef Pfeiffer had been the first one to start in this field when he took up the respective production in 1847.[3] This production line expanded specifically in the 1870s and the Riedels became largely involved in the making of "Rocailles" as well.

[1] Jargstorf, 1993:65
[2] ibid.:67
[3] ibid.:120

## Gablonz and its bead industry

Another famous Gablonz dynasty joined in the bead business in this period. The Ludwig Breit factory in Wiesenthal, which had been founded around 1870, produced tubes as well as "Rocailles." The Breit company expanded continually and in 1912 they inaugurated a new bead factory. After World War I they not only produced tubes for their own beadmaking, but canes for other local makers as well.

Another important branch of the Gablonz bead industry was lampworking beads - with two major subbranches, beadblowing and beadmolding. Beadblowing was taken up in the late 18th century. During the first third of the 19th century, blown beads were reckoned among the most profitable export items from the Gablonz industry. The makers developed many different methods for producing an endless variety of those beads during the first half of the 19th century. In addition to the luxury beads which were blown individually from the finest colored composition (a glass rich in lead) and decorated with painted ornaments, the makers blew standard beads from colorless crystal which were colored by a simple lining. Around 1874, productivity in this branch also was considerably improved through the

Four strands of blown beads from Gablonz, early twentieth century. According to old records the blown beads of the early nineteenth century had even more fancy and elaborate shapes. The upper strand with the green beads includes again two mother-of-pearl beads. This extremely attractive variety of blown beads was made until the early twentieth century.

use of blowing molds which allowed the beadblower to produce up to eight beads simultaneously. The two major design lines among those blown beads were artificial pearls and beads with metal lining. Between 1880 and 1885 the demand for metal-lined beads grew so high that the area supported approximately 2000 beadblowers. In addition to the standard "mirror" beads with a silver-colored lining - a bead type which had been produced since the 18th century - the Weiskopf company from Morchenstern introduced gold-lined beads in the second half of the 19th century - a variety which became one of the greatest successes of the Gablonz bead industry.[1]

In drawn beads and blown beads, the Gablonzers offered with a few exceptions, hardly any designs which were not also produced elsewhere. Yet their range in fancy pressmolded beads remained unequalled. Their entire industry had more or less grown out of this technique, a new procedure in the 18th century which allowed for higher productivity than the techniques used by others, causing important production lines to withdraw from other European glass industries. Pressmolding is abundantly documented in the second half of the 18th century in and around Gablonz.[2] The first pressmolded products were pendants for chandeliers and small bottles - both extremely well selling products on the fashionable markets. This high demand caused the tremendous success of the new production mode.

It is not recorded when exactly the Gablonz makers started to pressmold beads - but such beads were included in the selection of beads which the Gablonzers exposed at the 1829 exhibition in Prague, where the various Bohemian manufacturers/merchants displayed their finest achievements - mainly made by cottage workers whose exploitation guaranteed the unbeatably low prices!

The type of lampworked beads which dominated in Murano and Venice had been made in this area since at least the late 18th century, but they never played such an important role (quantity-wise) as they did in Italy.

[1]Jargstorf, 1993:36 + 58
[2]ibid.:49/50

Red, orange, and yellow beads, possibly Gablonz, 20th century (Thomas Morbe, Frankfurt).

## "Swarovski" beads

Fully faceted crystal beads were most likely the leading production line of the Gablonz bead industry. Such faceted beads in gem-colors like ruby, topaz, or emerald reckoned among the oldest design lines in beads and were already being produced in the first half of the 18th century. Their production is closely linked to the making of artificial gems which had been introduced in the area during the early 18th century.[1] No written reference to this very early bead production exists, but one can find rosaries composed mainly of garnet-colored faceted beads which can be attributed to this period and origin. Those early faceted glass beads were made in the same way as the stone beads; the bead was cut from a broken piece of glass and a hole was drilled.

The making of such gems (and beads) was simplified in the second half of the 18th century by pressmolding them initially, reducing the necessary cutting work. In the same way as pressmolding had almost been an industrial revolution which rose productivity in this field very abruptly, a further industrial revolution in the 1880s brought about the total mechanization of standard faceted gems and beads. One leading and most inventive manufacturer in this period was Daniel Swarovski, who originated from Gablonz and moved to Tyrol in 1895.[2] He applied machine faceting to artificial gems and during the 20th century also became a leading supplier of faceted beads.

[1]Jargstorf, 1993:33
[2]ibid.:44

A list of Austrian glass bead manufacturers/merchants in 1888. Nothing better illustrates the world leadership of Gablonz's bead production at the end of the nineteenth century then this list in a French directory of the glass industry. The list includes ninety-eight companies in Austria - and sixty of them are located in the Gablonz area!

Christmas decorations assembled from drawn and blown beads and bugles into spidernets and spiders, Gablonz, 1930s/40s. The Christmas decorations from Thuringia are generally rather large blown items while the Gablonzers created such fanciful assemblies. Some among the beads are quite elaborate such as the beads which form the body of the spiders yet the others are very standard beads.

## A new beginning

Bohemia became part of the newly founded Czechoslovakian Republic in 1918. After World War II, the Gablonzers were expulsed from North Bohemia, as they were of German descent. The existing bead factories passed under Czech control. As the Czech complement of Gablonz - Zeleny Brod - had been considerably strengthened by support from the administration in Prague since the 1920s, and as the lampworking of beads in the Venetian manner had always been largely in the hands of Czech cottage workers, the local bead industry didn't suffer as much from this disruption as the rest of the Gablonz jewelry industry.

"Bohemian" beadmaking was continued after the war in Jablonec (Gablonz) and in various places above all in Austria and Germany, where the expelled German-Bohemians settled and tried to rebuild their industry. Neugablonz in Bavaria became the most important location of this new industry.

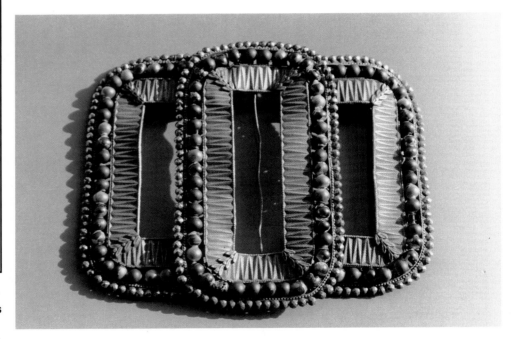

A "Biedermeier" buckle including blown and lined beads from Gablonz, early nineteenth century.

Two necklaces with blue faceted beads from Gablonz, 1930s. The necklaces are arranged upon two typical specimens of the Bohemian glass industry in the early nineteenth century; a cobalt-blue beaker and an alabaster glass vase with blue overlay and intricate cutting. The Bohemian glass industry had been inspired with its wonderful colors and also with its techniques by the beadindustry.

Three necklaces from Gablonz, 1930s. The necklaces include standard silver-lined beads. The beads on two necklaces appear to be gold-lined yet they are just made from topaz-colored glass.

Christmas decorations assembled from drawn and blown beads, Gablonz, 1930s/40s. Small standard beads are assembled into a butterfly and an insect. Thuringian Christmas decorations were generally closely related to Christmas as the glass was blown into such items as angels or Santa Clauses while those Bohemian decorations represented all types of subjects.

Four strands including blown beads, "Sprengperlen" and drawn bugles, Gablonz, late nineteenth century. The blue drawn and blown beads are made of blue glass while the rest of the beads is silver-lined and color-lined.

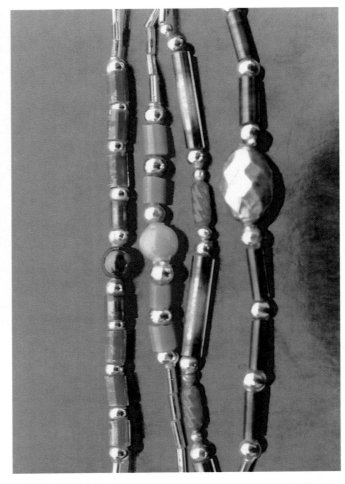

A necklace with blown beads from Gablonz, 1930s. Blown beads remained a major production line of the Gablonz bead industry up to the 1930s. The procedures for making them were perfected and their designs developed into an unimaginable variety. This necklace includes quite standard silver-lined beads. The beads are molded with facets and they are blown from yellow glass and thus they appear to be golden beads. The necklace also includes very elaborate bright yellow beads which are decorated with lampworked white dots.

Christmas decorations assembled from drawn and blown beads, Gablonz, 1930s/40s. These beads have been assembled into a motorbike and a car.

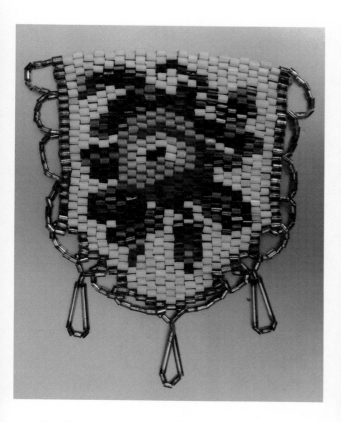

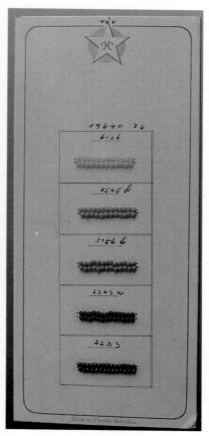

A sample card of "Rocailles" - the small beads cut from round tubes and rounded at the ends by reheating - company Fried Frères, Gablonz, 1930s. These beads have not only extremely fine colors - such as "coral," "turquoise," and "lapis," - but they excel also in their perfectly round shape.

Beadwork assembled of drawn beads from Gablonz, nineteenth century (Glass Museum Neugablonz).

The representation of the company Jäckel from Gablonz in Lagos/Nigeria, early twentieth century. The Gablonz bead industry had plenty of representations in Africa and the Jäckel company was specifically involved in the African trade.

An assembly of "Sprengperlen" and blown beads from Gablonz, nineteenth century (Glass Museum Neugablonz). The blue, the moss-green, and the white beads are drawn from mother-of-pearl glass. The other beads are silver-lined and color-lined yet in four cases the silver-lining had been applied to colored glass.

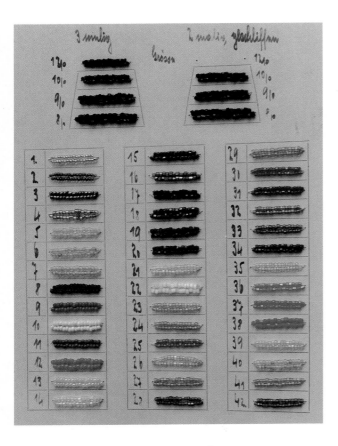

A sample card including drawn beads from Gablonz, early twentieth century. This sample card shows the many variations of small drawn beads which were made in Gablonz: Beads made of round tubes or 6-sided tubes, Beads made of colored glass or of clear glass lined with color. Beads with a fine sheen made of mother-of-pearl glass or of common glass with a luster coating, and last but not least, beads which had been cut and polished in addition to give them extra sparkle.

A necklace including fancy lampworked beads, Gablonz, 1930s.

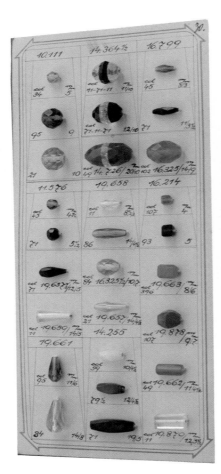

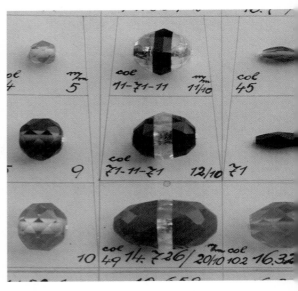

A sample card with faceted beads from Gablonz, first third of the twentieth century. This sample card shows some special varieties among the faceted beads, i.e. some uncommon shapes and some unusual colors such as the rose and the amethyst shades.

Close-up on the sample card. A very special and elaborate variety among the faceted beads from Gablonz were the beads which are combined from two colors of glass such as the beads in the middle row.

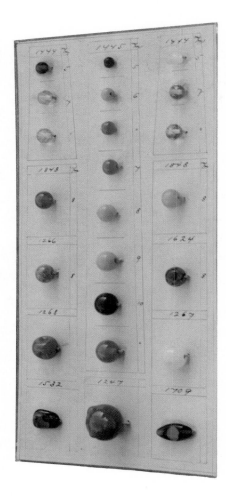

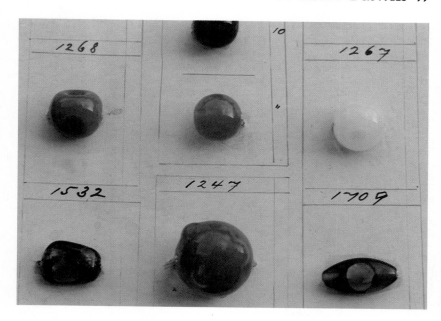

Close-up of the sample card showing two elaborate beads (1532 and 1709) with foil inclusions. The left bead is combined from blue and green glass and the right bead includes green, blue, and red glass.

A sample card including lampworked beads from Gablonz, 1920s/30s.

Letter-head of the bead manufacturer Adolf Wenzel from Gablonz in the 1920s. This letter head gives an idea into which enormous size the bead industry from Gablonz had grown in the early 20th century. A. Wenzel represented but one among many companies.

Three necklaces with lampworked beads from Gablonz, 1930s. Some among the beads are standard round, barrel-shaped, and melon-shaped beads yet some are very unusual with their fancy lampworked pattern.

A necklace with interlocking beads from Gablonz, 1930s. Various types of interlocking beads were a typical production line of the Gablonz bead industry.

A sample card including lampworked beads from Gablonz, 1920s/30s. These beads appear to be standard round beads yet they are made of exceptional gem-colored glass, including the shades "coral," "hematite," "lapis," "carnelian," and "chrysoprase."

An eye-catching necklace with the typical bead patterns and strong color contrasts of the 1930s from Gablonz.

A sample card with "porcelain" beads from Gablonz, 1930s. The sample card shows the various sizes and shapes of those beads.

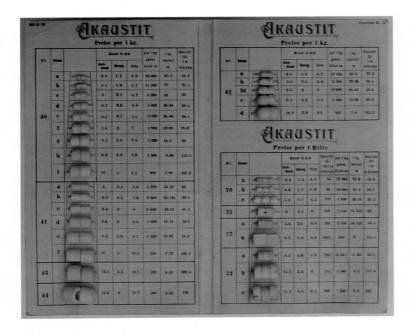

A fashionable necklace of the 1930s,
uncertain origin. The rose-colored beads
on this necklace are "porcelain" beads.

A necklace composed of pressmolded
beads from Gablonz, 1930s. The large
beads and some of the small beads are
made of "ice" glass which is glass with
internal fractures. These beads were very
fashionable in the 1920s and 1930s.

Two necklaces with lampworked "flower"
beads, possibly Zeleny Brod, 1930s/40s.
Such fancy lampworking was a speciality of
the Czech beadmakers who also made
imaginative lampworked figurines.

A table mat composed of "porcelain" beads, Germany, 1930s. The very cheap "porcelain" beads were generally worked into such useful items.

A necklace from modern Morocco including some "porcelain" beads. Such necklaces in traditional patterns are sold to the tourists. They are composed of locally-made beads such as the barrel-shaped green beads and generally quite standard imported beads. The silver pendant was made in Morocco as well. All glass beads on this necklace are "porcelain" beads except for the yellow-and-white overlay beads.

Lampworking beads in the 1950s in Germany. The finished beads are still on the copper wire. The metal is stuck into a pot which is filled with sand. Thus they can cool down.

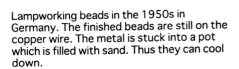

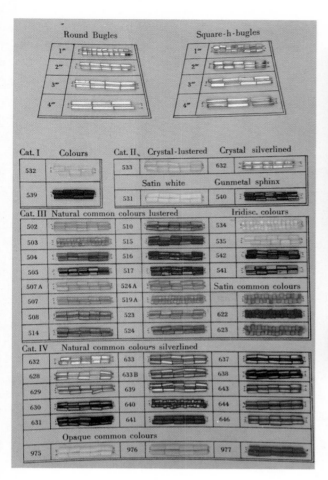

| Round Bugles | | Square-h-bugles | |
|---|---|---|---|
| 1" | | 1" | |
| 2" | | 2" | |
| 3" | | 3" | |
| 4" | | 4" | |

| Cat. I | Colours | | Cat. II | Crystal-lustered | | Crystal silverlined | |
|---|---|---|---|---|---|---|---|
| 532 | | | 533 | | | 632 | |
| | | | | Satin white | | Gunmetal sphinx | |
| 539 | | | 531 | | | 540 | |

| Cat. III | Natural common colours lustered | | | | | Iridisc. colours | |
|---|---|---|---|---|---|---|---|
| 502 | | 510 | | | 534 | | |
| 503 | | 515 | | | 535 | | |
| 504 | | 516 | | | 542 | | |
| 505 | | 517 | | | 541 | | |
| 507 A | | 524A | | | Satin common colours | | |
| 507 | | 519A | | | 622 | | |
| 508 | | 523 | | | 622 | | |
| 514 | | 524 | | | 623 | | |

| Cat. IV | Natural common colours silverlined | | | | | | |
|---|---|---|---|---|---|---|---|
| 632 | | 633 | | | 637 | | |
| 628 | | 633 B | | | 638 | | |
| 629 | | 639 | | | 643 | | |
| 630 | | 640 | | | 644 | | |
| 631 | | 641 | | | 646 | | |

| Opaque common colours | | | | | |
|---|---|---|---|---|---|
| 975 | | 976 | | 977 | |

A sample card with bugles and beads from Jablonec, 1950s/60s. The Czech bead industry produces very fine "Rocailles" and bugles.

Two modern necklaces from Zeleny Brod, 1991.

The Harz Mountains/Germany in the early 1920s. Some of the expulsed Gablonzers settled in various places around the Harz Mountains after the war and rebuilt a glass and jewelry industry there.

A necklace with lampworked beads "in the Venetian manner" from Jablonec/Zeleny Brod, modern.

A set of earpendants from the USA, 1992. The lampworked beads are from Jablonec/Zeleny Brod. The modern lampworkers continue a pattern which dates back to the late nineteenth century with these beads (see page 150).

Two necklaces from Jablonec, 1970s. These necklaces reproduce a standard pattern of the 1930s.

Pressmolded beads from Quedlinburg/Harz Mountains, 1950s. The first post-war beads were made in the traditional patterns of the pre-war period therefore it is sometimes very difficult to attribute the "Bohemian" beads correctly.

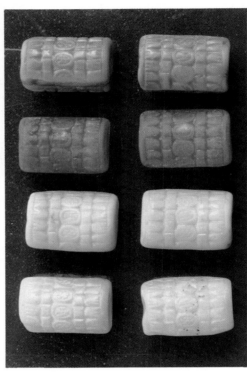

Pressmolded beads from Quedlinburg/Harz Mountains, 1950s.

## Euro-African Trade

### "There should not be any trade of slaves" (King Alfonso of Congo, 1526)

Since the 12th century, the Genoese had tried to enter this "new" world in order to have their share in the high profit rates of the African trade. They had fought successfully to obtain a base on the North African coast, but the Arabs prevented their further progress into the continent, thus they tried in vain to make their entrance via the sea. Several attempts to sail along the West African coast are known to have been made - but the valiant sailors never returned. The major obstacle was the winds; it was not until the early 15th century that the Europeans were capable of sailing into wind. But having learned the use of the Lateen sail from Arab sailors, and adopted further nautical devices, such as the compass and the astrolabe - which had been invented in China and had also reached the Europeans through the Arabs, a Portuguese crew sailed beyond Cap Bojador in 1434 - and returned safely! Other Europeans followed where the Portuguese had led.

The 16th century was a time of European rivalry and piracy along the West African coast, with the Portuguese claiming (in vain) a monopoly of access to West Africa by right of Papal bull. It was also a period of vain

A map of Africa in 1660. The map is almost correct as regards the coastal areas but it still includes the major errors about Inner Africa which existed in antiquity.

attempts by some African rulers to prevent slave trade who saw how their social system was being shattered by the sudden and overabundant flow of tempting "exotic," i.e. European, goods into their countries. King Alfonso of Congo supplicated the Portuguese king for not sending further merchants because "many of our subjects desirous of the wares of your kingdom seize many of our people and take them to be sold to the white men...but it is our will that in these kingdoms there should not be any trade of slaves," but we know that he was not successful.

## *"Sleight beades and blew corall" (1554)*

There are plenty of European (trade) records from the 16th century, which include lists of "the commodities that are most desired on the Guinean Coast," in which the glass beads had but a small share! Whenever those early merchants refer to the tokens of friendship they offered to the Africans, or the goods which they bartered for slaves, gold, ivory, and spices, they mention above all else textiles, weapons, tools, and metal ornaments.

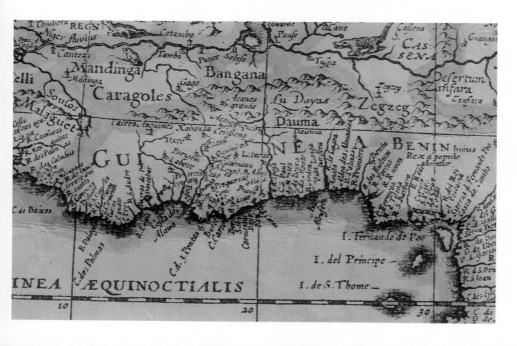

Close-up on the map showing the Guinean coast and the Portuguese stronghold São Jorge da Mina.

The exception to this rule was the area close to the Portuguese strongholds, such as their most important base on the West African coast, the fortress São Jorge da Mina. Here the Portuguese merchants had been distributing various (cheap) ornaments they knew from the East Coast trade, including Indian glass beads. The closer to the Portuguese forts the other Europeans traded, the more successful they were in bartering beads. Because they were in permanent fear of violent Portuguese attacks, they tried to find independent approaches to the Africans, as the English Merchant Adventurers attempted, "on their second voyage to Guinea in the yere 1554," only to make the disappointing discovery that Africans who were not yet Europeanized held no esteem at all for their glass beads.[1]

[1]Hakluyt, no date, volume IV:83

### "Stuffes and beades" (Joao dos Santos, 1600)

Medieval Portugal was a small impoverished country which felt - along with other European countries - deplorably restricted by the commercial dominance of the Islamic world. The Arabs controlled not only the African trade but also the luxury trade with the Far East. The main scope of Portugal's imperial adventure was the search for the sources of Arabian gold and the ardent desire to get direct access to the lucrative trade with India and China.

For European industries and manufacturers, Vasco da Gama opened new horizons but for the Africans, his coming meant disaster! His compatriots brutally ended a flourishing epoch of untrammeled trading between the African kingdoms and empires such as Persia, India, and China - a trade to the mutual benefit of each partner. In 1500 the first Portuguese fleet dropped anchor off Kilwa, the town which the cosmopolitan Ibn Battuta had praised as being one of the most beautiful towns in the world, and which the Portuguese royal agent Duarte Barbosa admired for its architectural perfection around 1500, which in his eyes resembled a southern Venice. In 1505 the city was sacked, plundered, and replaced by a Portuguese garrison. As most cities on the east coast "moved by arrogance, refused to obey the king our Lord" (in the words of Barbosa), they were taken by force, plundered, and eventually pulled down "as their maintenance was of no value nor profit."

The Portuguese soon became aware that they depended upon inland powers in their quest for gold. The Swahili merchants, whose cities they had taken control of, were anything but anxious to enlighten them about the sophisticated trading network that had been in operation for centuries. Thus the Portuguese made erratic attempts to get direct access to the precious metal but succeeded only in undermining the social systems they had found.

It appears that the Portuguese considerably reduced the once spectacular range of goods which had been imported into African kingdoms. Around 1600, Joao dos Santos, a Dominican priest who was living on the east coast, repeatedly reported that his compatriots traded but "stuffes and beades." The Dutch of the 17th century - such as the famous Olfert Dappert - confirmed this deterioration in the quality of the goods bartered by the Europeans. The South Africans received mostly tobacco, brandy, and ornaments such as Indian glass beads and copper bracelets and beads in exchange for their own "riches"; such as cattle. The entire view of the Africans changed deplorably with the advent of the Europeans and the same Dutch reporters who considered it worth reporting that sexual intercourse with an AmaXhosa woman was obtainable for ten glass beads.

São Jorge da Mina in 1660. This fortress was the main military and trading post of the Portuguese in West Africa.

## "The chiefest trade consists in slaves" (James Barbot, 1701)

Until the end of the 16th century Portugal was more or less able to maintain the monopoly of the West African trade. There were sporadic voyages by English and French interlopers, but it was only the Dutch who set out, in the last third of the 16th century, to destroy this supremacy. By 1610, the Dutch had driven the Portuguese out of the East Indies, and by 1642 all the Portuguese forts on the Gold Coast were under Dutch control.

The trading records of the 17th century are mainly concerned with European rivalry in their run for African riches and with their involvement with the slave trade. They had not yet found direct access to African gold, and they did not know about the other profitable goods which Africa offered - such as palm-oil - and thus "the chiefest trade" of the Europeans consisted in slaves.

Around 1680, an agent of the French African companies transcribed very detailed lists "as to the different sorts of goods the Europeans generally carry thither for trade." We learn from him that each of the nations now mainly involved in the African trade - the Dutch, French, and English - carried, among other goods such as textiles, tools, weapons, brandy, large cylindrical beads and other beads "of sundry colors and sizes" to the Gold Coast to purchase slaves and, eventually, some gold dust. The English, as well as the French, got their beads from the Dutch but this is no indication of their true place of origin, because we know that every important bead producer sent his beads to the Netherlands for further export. Only the large cylindrical beads are mentioned separately and were apparently a "Venetian" specialty.

## Prussian beads for West Africa

Since the mid-17th century the Prince Friedrich-Wilhelm of Brandenburg - an area which was to become the central province of Prussia in 1701 - had attempted to found a trading company similar to the Dutch-East-India company, hoping to thus improve the economy of his country, which suffered severely from Swedish predominance in and around the Baltic. In 1682, the Brandenburg-African company was finally founded. But the sea powers of England and the Netherlands fought with every possible means against the colonial aspirations of Brandenburg/Prussia, and in 1720 the German trading base in Africa had to be sold to the Netherlands.

The famous glassmaker and alchemist Johann Kunckel (1620/30 - 1703), who had been in the services of the Brandenburg Prince since 1678, made not only exceptional blown glass, but glass beads (Glas-korallen) as

Four Rosetta beads from Murano, various periods (Jürgen Busch, Germany). Modern Rosetta beads have a standard shape with rounded ends and a standard amount of six layers. In the past the Rosetta canes sometimes had more and sometimes less then six layers and they had important variations in the color sequence within the canes. The beads had also various shapes; for example, cut at the ends like the beads depicted here.

well.[1] The Brandenburg-African company had an option on this bead production and traded the beads to the Guinean coast. Kunckel had specialized in Potsdam/Brandenburg on fine colored glass and he had perfected gold-ruby glass. He made faceted beads in the corresponding colors.[2] With those types of beads the Prussian traders may have even initiated the appreciation of such faceted beads in certain areas of West Africa.

[1]Keramische Rundschau 3/1910:29
[2]Pazaurek, 1911:7/8

## Jaja, King of Opobo

The 17th century had brought the first crucial changes for African societies. The Europeans had opened the back-door to West Africa and thus the inner African kingdoms lost monopoly of trade as commerce shifted towards the Guinean coast. After the collapse of such powers as the Songhay Empire at the end of the 16th century the Sudan suffered two centuries of political disunity. The trans-Sahara-trade dwindled and the once flourishing trading capitals such as Timbuktu and Djenné became impoverished. New coastal powers started to rise in the late 17th century, such as the Ashanti confederacy or the kingdom of Benin. Their rise was well supported by European muskets and carabins. But despite such "help" they were anything but docile trading partners to the Europeans. The Africans continued to control all aspects and steps of the commercial exchange - and above all they continued to prevent access to their gold mines! A close commercial bond existed between the inland suppliers and the coastal middleman and the policy of the middleman was to isolate the European traders on their moored ships. Because England and France had started to foster a "national" trade in the 17th century, their helpless dependance nourished the idea that (military) force was a necessary prerequisite to "orderly" commerce - but the encroachment of the European powers was met with fierce resistance. Yet the Europeans later found other means to impose their will, and Jaja, King of Opobo, was a famous victim of European legalism. He controlled the palm-oil trade in the second half of the 19th century in the Niger delta region by protecting his sources of supply and by fixing the prices at which he was willing to sell. The British government reacted to this "unlawful" behavior by convicting and deporting him to the West Indies in 1887.

## "I mezzi di far rifiorire il commercio delle conterie" (=how to improve the bead trade) (Gasparo Gozzi, 1761)

The Venetian bead industry was in a deep crisis around the mid-18th century. Among other problems, it was not able to match the rising demand for glass beads, which, according to some records had suddenly almost doubled.[1] The main export of the Venetian bead industry in former periods had gone to the Levantine markets. As this demand considerably slackened, the manufacturers reduced their output and the number of workers to keep prices stable, but were gradually unable to satisfy their commissions and lost market shares to bead industries north of the Alps. In 1754, a chronicler deplored that the few manufacturers which monopolized production were not willing to allow new manufacturers to start business and that certain workers - equally protected by the guild laws - were unwilling to work harder.[2]

Yet however great the demand for beads might have been, glass beads did not play a leading role among goods shipped to Africa. In this century the "Top Ten" were products such as Danish guns, French muskets, gunpowder, French brandy, Barbados rum, Dutch linen, Leyden serges,

A bronze plastic representing a princess from the kingdom of Benin, Nigeria, eighteenth century. The princess is adorned with abundant beadwork and a string of large bugles around her waist. In these early periods the use of the "exotic" European glass beads was still restricted in many African societies to the upper classes or to special (religious) purposes.

Indian callicoes, and pans and dishes. Glass beads ranked far below such "useful" goods. In most parts of Africa they were still far from having replaced the traditional ornaments such as metal beads and ivory bracelets. An important reason for this was the fact that the trade was still fully controlled by the African leaders, who took care to restrict access to foreign and thus valuable ornaments whenever possible, just as the Europeans at home were still severely hampered by law regarding their way of dressing. "Exotic" glass beads were still restricted to very special use in Africa. As in our societies honor and advancement is often linked to a medal - which is basically nothing but a piece of metal - the king of Benin likewise used a string of glass beads. Since the 17th century, records repeatedly tell of the "Coral-Feast," where during a splendid celebration the Oba of Benin bestowed a string of beads on those whose position he advanced.

[1]Cucchetti, 1884:1
[2]ibid.:9

Blue cylindrical beads, possibly Gablonz or Murano, possibly 19th century (Thomas Morbe, Frankfurt). Such drawn beads are mostly attributed to Bohemia yet this type of bead was made up to the 19th century in Murano as well.

Overlay beads, possibly Gablonz or Murano, 19th/20th century. (Thomas Morbe, Frankfurt) Related compound beads were found in excavation sites of the two Americas. They were named "Nueva Cadiz" beads after one such site in an island off Venezuela. It was a Spanish port in the first half of the 16th century. Those beads are generally dated to the 16th and 17th centuries. Similar small overlay beads were also found in excavation sites near Timbuktu/Africa. The origin of those early Nueva Cadiz beads has not yet been ascertained. Based on the Ximenes-Neri correspondence (see page 73) and on Dutch glass finds including fragments of blown glass decorated with cane segments identical to the Nueva Cadiz canes I would strongly suspect a Dutch origin or possibly a Pisane origin - the latter specifically because of the Genoese (and Pisane) involvement with the North African trade. "Nueva Cadiz" cane segments dating from about 1575 were excavated in Antwerp (see page 71). They were presumably made in the area. The modern Nueva Cadiz beads on the picture have in common with the old beads only the square shape and the dominant colors i.e., either blue or green as well as the small white layer which was once included for no other reason than to give the outer colors more brilliance, as the glassmakers still had much difficulty in achieving a fine transparent and brilliant red and blue.

## "Christianity, commerce, colonization..."(slogan of the abolitionist movement)

Up to the 19th century the contact with the Europeans had cost the Africans well over 14 million of their people. In this century, European interest in Africa took a new turn: "legitimate" trade became the new (British) keyword - after the European explorers revealed the gigantic resources which the African continent held for European industries. To prevent that the Africans

A part of a map showing the Guinean coast in 1743. The map is illustrated with West African fashions showing fine textiles, important headgear and a rather restricted amount of beaded jewelry. These were the main characteristics of the upper class fashions in many regions of West Africa.

would dictate the terms of trade in this big deal, European churches and racism joined forces to justify overthrowing the entire continent, claiming it was "the white man's burden" to let the future of the Africans be fully determined by the Europeans.

The trading contact between Europe and Africa took on new dimensions in the colonial period, whose official beginning was the international "share out" conference of 1884/85 in Berlin. Gigantic quantities of raw materials from Africa made the European industries expand and large quantities of European industrial goods poured into the African markets - among them various kinds of glass beads. No African ruler could restrict their use anymore; beads became freely available and began to considerably influence fashions and costumes. Beaded adornments such as the impressive beaded corsets of the Dinka or the huge beaded necklaces and bracelets of the Ndebele are the products of such abundance - while the traditional ornaments of the Dinka closely resembled those of the "White Lady of Auanrhet" (see page 20).

We might get a faint idea of the incredible masses of beads which arrived since about the second half of the 19th century in Africa if we look at nothing but the ports of the small German colonial empire in East Africa in a single year. They imported in 1896[1]:

| Provenance | Weight in British pounds |
| --- | --- |
| Germany | 41,525 |
| Bohemia | 105,233 |
| Murano/Venice | 79,426 |
| India | 1,022 |
| China | 26,963 |
| Japan | 10,646 |

These figures also inform us of the standard provenances of African glass beads around 1900.

[1] Deutsches Kolonialblatt, Berlin, 15. April 1897

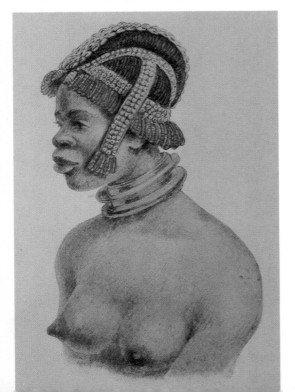

Elaborate beaded hairdo from Inner Africa, early twentieth century. The ornament includes cowrie shells and white and red cylindrical beads.

A map showing the Prussian base "Gross Friedrichsburg" on the Guinean coast. This early Prussian involvment with colonialism lasted only for a few years in the seventeenth/eighteenth century. The Germans were soon driven out of this continent by the leading (colonial) powers. Yet in this short period they possibly initiated the West African taste for transparent faceted beads.

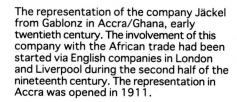

The representation of the company Jäckel from Gablonz in Accra/Ghana, early twentieth century. The involvement of this company with the African trade had been started via English companies in London and Liverpool during the second half of the nineteenth century. The representation in Accra was opened in 1911.

Lampworking in the 17th century Germany. Johann Kunckel commented and extended Neri's "L'Arte Vetraria." Kunckel's "Ars Vitraria" or "Glasmacherkunst," which was published for the first time in 1679, included a chapter on lampworking while Neri's didn't refer to lampworking. Three men are lampworking on Kunckel's picture and one among them is twisting a cane. Kunckel refers in the text to blowing glass-globes to be filled either with various items - figurines, crucifixes, etc. - or to be lined with colors. He refers also to lampworking chemical utensils (Kunckel was by profession a chemist!) He doesn't mention lampworking beads! None of the lampworkers on the picture are making beads. The tiny bits in the middle of the table are just broken bits of (lead) glass with which the lampworkers started their work. They did not yet necessarily start with tubes or canes, as is modern practice. From Kunckel's extension we can learn indirectly that drawing canes and tubes was common practice in (North) European glassworks.

Six elaborate beads from Mauretania, twentieth century (Courtesy of Jürgen Busch, Germany). The Africans had their own traditions in artificial beads which were largely based on elaborate metal beads yet some records of the past tell equally about African glass beadmaking. The most splendid documents of African glass bead art are certainly these beads from Mauretania. They are made according to a very time-consuming method. Presently they are very much sought after by the bead collectors of the world - but in the past such African bead art was given little chance to grow or to survive. They could not compete with the tons of European glassbeads which poured into this continent.

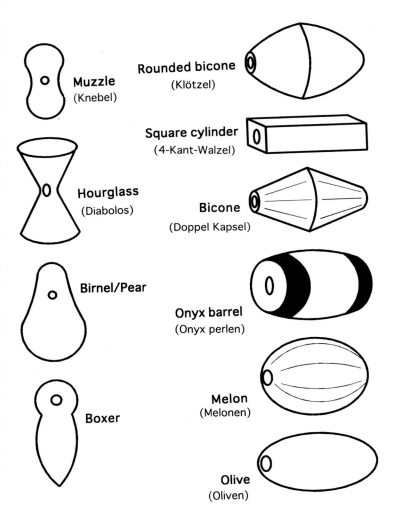

**Muzzle** (Knebel)

**Hourglass** (Diabolos)

**Birnel/Pear**

**Boxer**

**Rounded bicone** (Klötzel)

**Square cylinder** (4-Kant-Walzel)

**Bicone** (Doppel Kapsel)

**Onyx barrel** (Onyx perlen)

**Melon** (Melonen)

**Olive** (Oliven)

The basic bead types from Gablonz which were made for the African trade.

Molded beads from Gablonz, 20th century (Thomas Morbe, Frankfurt).
These beads were originally named "Birnel" (=pear). Among American bead collectors they got the designation "teardrop."

Four leather strings with beads from the African trade. The beads are from Murano, twentieth century. Those beads had been traded during many decennia into Africa and got little attention elsewhere. In the 1960s/70s they were "discovered" by the protesting youth in North America and Europe and such "ethno-look" necklaces became a standard adornment.

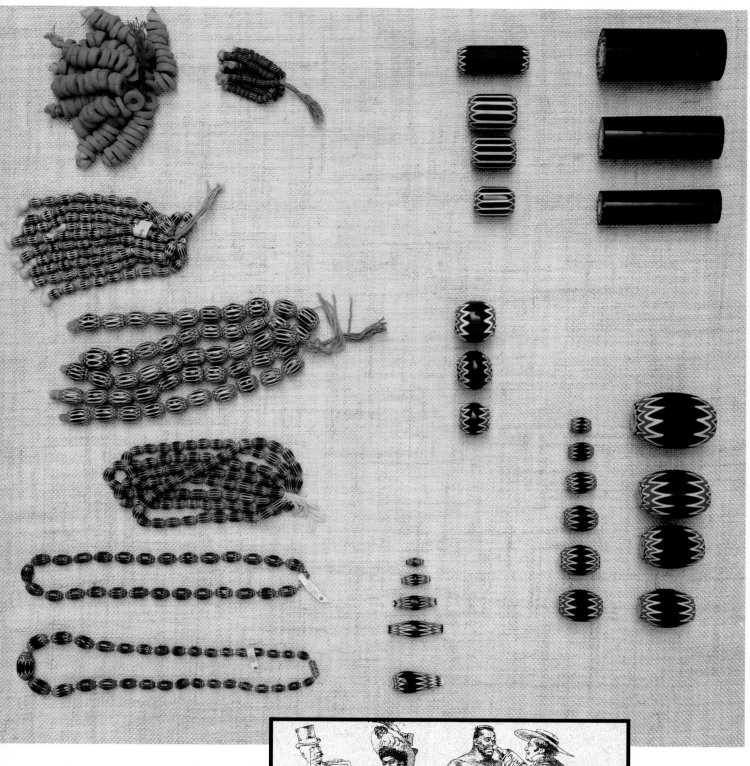

Various Rosetta beads of the E. Moretti & f.lli company from Murano, twentieth century (Courtesy of E. Moretti & f.lli).

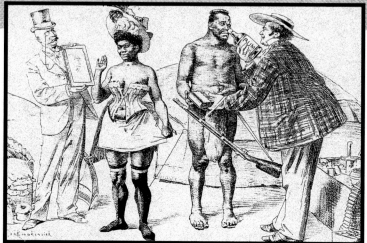

A Dutch caricature of 1897, attacking the European exploitation of the Africans.

An elaborate necklace from South Africa, twentieth century. Many traditional African patterns are expressed with the never fading brilliance of glass beads.

Yoruba-beadwork from West Africa, twentieth century. The Yoruba created most imaginative yet quite naturalistic beadwork including such motifs as human faces.

A costume doll from South Africa, ornamented with beadwork. Many items which are made for the tourists include plenty of beadwork.

Yoruba-beadwork from West Africa, twentieth century. Animals are a frequently used motif in Yoruba beadwork.

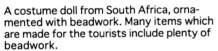

## Paying beads

Beads are often said to have been the African currency. In reality, beads were as much an African currency as "Lucky Strikes" were German currency during the post-war years. Both goods were very much desired and quite helpful for bartering but never became a real currency - this held true in Africa at least as long as the Africans succeeded in maintaining some of their political and social independence. Africa had basically the same systems for trading as Europe - either a pure bartering system or a trade based upon currencies. Early currencies were gold or copperbased - as Al Hassan ibn Muhammed al-Wizaz al-Fasi described it in the mid-16th century: "The coine of Tombuto (=Timbuktu) is of gold without any stampe or superscription. In matter of small value they use certaine shels brought hither out of the kingdom of Persia, four hundred of which shels are worth a ducate"[1].

The Africans later adopted certain European currencies, such as the Maria-Theresia-Thaler from Austria. Many European explorers of the 19th century reported that this "Thaler" was absolutely indispensable for travelling Africa, apparently a "key" currency. The cowrie shell remained through all these periods the small coin. In the mid-19th century the German explorer Barth tells of the "most boring and tiresome shell-counting which is an indispensable element of trading in these countries. In this area (between the west coast and Lake Chad) the shells are not assembled by hundreds as on the east coast but have to be counted one by one." Barth was present when an African "with the help of five companions accomplished the heroic task of counting 500,000 shells."[2]fn

When trading according to the bartering system, the Europeans had to compose a complex package of European goods in order to obtain African ones. It was often very tiresome to compose a package which satisfied the African trading partner. We know from 1860s Gaboon that a package for buying ivory had to comprise thirty different European goods, among which the glass beads were a neglectable quantity, and in 1789 slaves were paid for with a package of goods comprised of guns, gunpowder, various

The colonial powers tried to introduce "real" currencies - such as these rupies of the German-Eastafrican bank in the early twentieth century.

A "Maria Theresia Thaler" of 1780 and some cowrie shells. This silver coin had been adopted in some areas of Africa as a standard currency. The cowrie shells used to be for centuries the small coins in many parts of Africa.

textiles and household goods, but no beads. The importance of glass beads within such a package could differ very much. Wherever European goods were still quite rare they were highly valued, but in areas "where the European merchants had long since introduced guns and powder and brandy and colorful textiles, the glass beads counted for nothing."[3]

Of course there were those isolated populations which reacted as enthusiastic to European glass beads as postwar Europeans did to American chewing gum - Africans which were ready to "sell" most precious African goods but for a handful of glass beads. But it is not justified to speak of an African bead "currency" because such common goods as food were frequently exchanged against such "exotic" goods as glass beads, or certain merchants succeeded in getting an elephant tusk for a copper bracelet or a string of beads from isolated, naive, and ignorant natives - while a similar tusk cost fifty Maria-Theresia-Thaler in the trading capitals along the Niger.[4]

[1] Africanus, 1896:824
[2] Barth, 1857:30-31
[3] Junkers, 1889:245
[4] Rohlf, 1868:84

A cowrie store in the early twentieth century. Some kings in Africa and in Southeast Asia had such cowrie stores and controlled thus the output of money. Some African kingdoms in the past had similar control and support mechanisms for their currencies as we do today.

# THE USE OF BEADS

*The whims of French fashions are most astonishing...the hairdoes rise - and suddenly they drop again. Their immense height can place the female face amidst her stature. In other periods her feet occupy this position as the enormous height of the heels rises them upon a pedestal. (Montesquieu [1686-1755] Les Lettres Persanes, letter XCIX)*

The famous "Persian letters" were meant to teach the Europeans a lesson about themselves. At any period they considered the fashions of the others to be strange, ridiculous or even immoral - always generously overlooking how ridiculous their own behavior was. The above text is the fictitious view of a young Persian on European mores - the text below represents the normal 19th century European view of African mores:

*The degraded condition of the women here was a depressing feature. Many of them are entirely unprotected by clothing of any kind, and, as if to make their appearance as hideous as possible, they have established the custom of tattooing their bodies.[1]*

Today our position has changed and African (beaded) costumes are admired for being strikingly exotic. Yet it might help for a better understanding not to dwell too extensively on the strange touch of African beaded fashions, but to look at the features they have in common with our own habits and costumes. I find considerable parallels between European and African costumes and their use of beads.

[1]Stanley in Africa, no date:271

King Munsa from the region of modern Sudan, 1870s. King Munsa considered only the products of African craftmanship adequate adornment and he categorically refused to wear European ornaments and beads.

## Controversial Beads

Europeans learned to appreciate glass beads as artistic ornaments only in the 20th century. Before this period, they were simply accepted as brilliant elements within a beaded ornament, otherwise considered proper for children and "savages." Even in Africa they were not met with general acceptance.

It was for their exotic rarity that made Africans, especially in the beginning of the bead trade, ready to pay their weight in gold - just as today we value certain beads, and are willing to pay a similar price for them: in 1993 a single Phoenician head bead fetched 8,050 British Pounds![1]

Besides this special desire for particular beads - which never affected the entire society in the past of Africa or in modern Europe, the Mer-

African hairdo in the 1910s. Throughout the centuries we can find written references to the sophisticated hairdoes in Africa. They were mostly ornamented until the nineteenth century either with cowrie shells or with metallic beads made by African craftsmen.

chant Adventurers of the 16th and 17th century and the explorers of the 18th and 19th century met with all sorts of responses to their glass beads - ranging from clear refusal to sheer enthusiasm. Early reports from the west coast tell of sumptuous ornaments which did not include any glass beads, and reveal a generally rather limited interest in glass beads. The English merchants can hardly believe in 1554 how the Africans "goe laden with collars, bracelets, hoopes and chaines, either of gold, copper or ivory"[2] combined to otherwise complete nakedness. On the east coast in 1498 Vasco da Gama wondered why a coastal chief did not value any of his gifts - neither the beads nor the bracelets - but asked instead for scarlet cloth, offering him in return a rosary(!).[3] The closer and the more frequent the contact with foreign merchants had been, the more glass beads gradually became integrated into African adornment. Thus Africans living close to the Portuguese strongholds on the western coast had adopted the fashion "to weare about their neckes great beades of glasse of diverse colours" by the mid-16th century.[4] When the first Dutch reached the Cape region in the first half of the 17th century they noted that the south Africans had also begun to replace the copper beads in the beadwork upon their skin dresses by Indian glass beads.[5] Later explorers noted their very clear opinion about the types of glass beads they wanted to have. When Le Vaillant offered them a large choice of colors in 1780, they took nothing but the white and red beads, declaring that the black and blue beads wouldn't go well with their skin.[6]

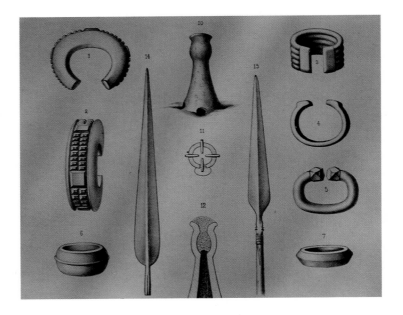

African brass and copper bracelets in 1875. Elaborate metal and Ivory ornaments dominated in Africa up to the nineteenth century.

Such request for specific types of beads gave the Europeans a lot of trouble. Thus James Bruce was deeply disappointed in 1769, when the Ethiopians strictly refused his "beautifully flowered beads" but required small blue beads and large yellow ones instead.[7] A German explorer met with equally specific demands about a hundred years later when in 1869 the Dinka wanted nothing but pea-sized white beads with blue dots and opalescent beads with one inch in diameter - refusing categorically any other bead.[8] We know already by Ximenes in 1603 about such precise demand - and the in addition permanently changing requests were a real nuisance for the traders. According to the German explorer Schweinfurth the stores of the Chartoum merchants were overflowing with out-of-fashion beads.

From the 16th century onwards, European glass beads became better known in more regions of Africa, but were not necessarily accepted as a valuable adornment. Among the Mangbattu, only the locally made ornaments - including copper beads - were considered adequate adornment for the king even as late as around 1870.[9] And a Prince of Madi refused to wear foreign jewelry, yet condescended to wear a string of large garnet-colored glass beads in order to please his European guests![10]

Many Europeans discovered a clear distinction between genuine beads and their glass substitutes among the Africans. Rohlfs reported from Kuka in the 1860s that most women desired many strings of coral and amber beads, and only the poor women would accept similar glass beads instead.[11] In a similar manner, the wealthy Bornu ladies of the 1870s wore coral, agate, and amber beads while the poor women had to be satisfied with glass. This attitude was even reflected in the terminology; high quality coral was named "mordschân" (German transcription), while the white heart beads - imitating coral - were named "mordschân talagabê (= "coral of the poor").

[1] Christie's: Ancient Egyptian glass III, London 8 December 1993, lot 153
[2] Hakluyt, no date, volume IV:62
[3] Ravenstein, 1898:139
[4] Hakluyt, no date, volume IV:86
[5] Schapera, 1933:37
[6] LeVaillant, 1790:221
[7] Hibbert, 1982:29
[8] Schweinfurth, 1922:79
[9] ibid.:312
[10] ibid.:230
[11] Rohlf, 1868:65

## Brilliant Beads

Glass beads are appreciated throughout the world for the practical reason that they are ideal for creating colorful ornaments on textiles. Since antiquity, textiles had been enhanced by embroidery work applied with threads and eventually incorporating some stones and beads. Glass beads offered striking advantages compared to other materials. They combined the qualities:
- A large choice of sizes,
- Regularity in size,
- Availability in large quantities,
- Brilliance that would not fade,
- An enormous choice of colors,
- Low price.

As soon as adequate glass beads became available, they were used in Europe as well as in Africa for traditional ornamentation, and began to replace the usual, inconvenient materials, such as silverthreads that would tarnish or natural beads with their annoying irregularity and high price.

Thus the Khoikhoi made their beadwork with glass instead of bronze beads, the Maasai adapted their customary metal collars to a new beaded version, and many other Africans replaced the cowrie shell with white beads. They were as thrilled about this brilliant element as Europeans in the 17th/18th century were about the silvery mother-of-pearl bugles or in the 1860s about the "gold" beads of Giacomuzzi (as golden and silvery ornaments were of central importance in European textile ornamentation).

A glass beaker decorated with beadwork, A. Meyr glassworks, Bohemian Forest, 1840 (Technisches Museum, Vienna). In this case the "Rocailles" replace the standard enameled decoration.

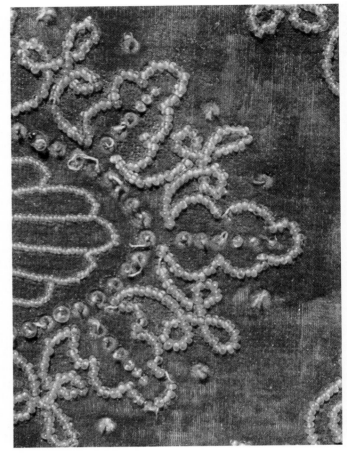

A table with beaded top from the workshop of J.M. van Selow, Braunschweig, second half of the eighteenth century (Courtesy of Städtisches Museum Braunschweig). In this case the beads were not used to replace fading embroidery work but as a handy substitute to minuscule mosaic elements.

A book cover with beaded ornaments, Venice, second half of the nineteenth century (Glass Museum, Murano). The beaded embroidery is made with the famous "gold" bead (perla giallo d'oro) which had been created by the bead manufacturer Giacomuzzi. Golden and silver embroidery work was always highly estimated in Europe and any bead reproducing those colors was much appreciated. Since the 17th century bead makers gave much thought to "gold" and "silver" beads and they created many types of such "metal" beads.

Russian beadwork, second half of the eighteenth century. The wonderful shiny effect is achieved with "Atlas" glass bugles. Even silk threads didn't match this brilliance and these beads were a welcomed substitute to silk and silver threads in embroidery work.

European beadwork and embroidery work with the typical romantic flower patterns of the nineteenth century. The never fading brilliance of the beadwork was a very appreciated advantage.

A beaded belt from Norway, nineteenth century and a Russian costume, nineteenth century, including a beaded necklace. The beaded items reproduce the patterns and the colors of the traditional embroidery work as it is found on the costume.

English beadwork of the 19th century. Typical home-made Victorian beadwork. Similar beadwork was made in almost every European country.

European beadwork of the nineteenth
century reproducing traditional patterns.

Traditional design from Cameroon,
nineteenth century, done in beadwork.

African beadwork, twentieth century,
reproducing the traditional Ndebele design
as it is also found on the walls of the houses.

Traditional patterns done in beadwork, East Africa, early twentieth century.

Yoruba beadwork from West Africa, nineteenth/twentieth century. Such naturalistic patterns are characteristic of the Yoruba design.

Modern African beadwork made for tourists. The beadwork reproduces traditional patterns yet the colors are not as carefully and meaningfully chosen as on the beadwork for African use.

Geometrical patterns in beadwork from South Africa, twentieth century, displayed on woven textiles from Zaire, nineteenth century. Extremely equilibrated geometrical patterns are a typical feature of African beadwork in many areas. The preference for such patterns derives possibly from the traditional patterns on woven textiles. Textile craft was highly developed in the past in many parts of Africa yet it perished as it couldn't compete with the cheap textiles from the European industries.

## Valuable Beads

Value is an extrinsic quality: what's rare is generally considered to be valuable. In the past, any foreign good could be regarded as rare and wearing such foreign goods was one way to profess high rank or "style." This tradition stems from antiquity to modern times - for example, from the Celtic upper classes who wore Mediterranean beads, to our modern habit of wearing rare "trade beads." In many societies this tendency to attempt to prove one's social position by wearing rare and foreign goods was even institutionalized: the many rigid costume laws in Europe functioned to stabilize social order, and in the Mapungubwe society (South-east Africa) in the 10th - 12th century "high status was signified by ownership and display of the rare and thus valuable trade goods from the Indian Ocean."[1] Our European upper-class costumes - which were strictly forbidden to common people - generally include plenty of exotic trade goods, such as Indian silk, Oriental beads, or African ivory. Eventually such goods were/are even made artificially rare. In our modern societies this applies to such "precious" goods as gold and diamonds, and in the 17th century in West Africa to the "blue coralls," large glass beads, which could have been largely available if the Oba of Benin would have allowed free trade.

Many Europeans considered the craze of certain Africans for cheap European glass beads rather childish behavior but considered their own craze for African ivory or Indian silk a most sincere matter, overlooking the identical pattern behind the two urgent desires.

As soon as the symbolic "value" of a certain good was accepted throughout a society, everybody strived to attain it - eventually, at any cost. The craze for these valuable symbols also created a large market for surrogates; such as the enormous market for artificial pearls in Europe and the quest for artificial corals in Africa.

[1]Hall, 1987:89

West African adorned with many necklaces including huge Rosetta beads, a symbol of rank.

A lady with important pearl jewelry. In European societies the pearls were hardly ever worn for the sole reason of their beauty but mostly to demonstrate wealth. Since at least the 14th century we can find plenty of costume laws in Europe prohibiting the middle classes from the pearl fashions of the upper classes.

Opalescent beads from Gablonz, early twentieth century. Opalescent beads were another variety of beads which was highly estimated in certain areas of Africa and...paid its weight in gold...

A lady with artificial pearls, Germany, 1928. A string of pearls was a standard dream of many a woman - yet most had to be happy with good quality artificial pearls.

Rosetta beads from Murano, various periods (Thomas Morbe, Frankfurt). The large beads are carefully rounded at the ends to reveal the pattern of the compound cane while most of the small beads are just cane segments. Only the oblong green beads are roughly faceted. European Rosetta beads meant to some Africans what the Oriental beads (pearls) meant to some Europeans: they were foreign, they were rare, they were expensive - and thus they were highly estimated!

Several necklaces with artificial pearls, Gablonz, first third of the twentieth century and Neugablonz, 1950s/60s. Such delicate "pearl" necklaces pretended to be the real thing.

Wall decoration from the burial site of Haremhab (1334-1306 BC) from Egypt. After a successful battle the general is honored by the Pharaoh Tutankhamun with many strands of beads.

A nineteenth century elephant mask from Cameroon (Völkerkunde Museum Leipzig). In the Bamileke society, elephants symbolize strength. As long as African rulers were able to restrict access to European beads in precolonial periods, such glassbeads represented wealth. The highly valued elephant motif and the "rare" beads taken together made beaded elephant masks an important mark of status.

A costume from Germany, nineteenth century. It is abundantly decorated with beaded embroidery. The dominance of the color blue indicates that this vest is part of the costume for a married woman.

## Symbolic Beads

Sometimes the quest for specific beads had a background related to the "valuable beads" mentioned above. In all societies certain colors have had strong symbolic value: they signalled to which social group a person belonged, or the role they had within the group. In the vanishing world of costumes, we can still find the last remnants of these social signals on both continents.

The attribution of social value to color was strongly reactivated in medieval Europe by the church, as the Catholic church was a leading political power with a major interest in maintaining social order. Such visible means of identification were adequate for the uneducated and illiterate majority of the European population. Pope Innocent III established the first such rules in 1200 which were repeatedly confirmed by later councils. Besides making black the color of mourning and white the color of the virgin (Mary), those rules established a social rank: gold and silver colors were reserved to the highest personalities, brilliant colors of any shade were the privilege of nobility, while the common people were restricted to wearing grey, brown, and black.

It was not easy for the high and mighty to maintain their color privileges, as the fine dyeing of textiles remained a great problem in Europe up to the 17th century and the Europeans had to largely rely upon beautifully colored Oriental textiles. Another substitute was the home-made embroidery work with Indian silk threads, but even that faded. European glass beads were a most welcome means of decorating dresses colorfully and brilliantly beginning in the late 16th century.

The "royal red" had a very special position among these color signals. Since antiquity, it had been linked to the highest social rank. In Europe as well as in certain African societies - such as the kingdom of Benin - it became the royal color, and consequently became the most coveted color on both continents. Each ascending class in Europe fought fiercely for the permission to use this "noble" color. In the 16th century, university professors were the first ones to gain this privilege, and in the 19th century it finally made its entrance into European costumes. Here it became the symbol of youth and the privileged color in the costume of the unmarried girl and the bride, hence a profusion of red beads generally decorate these respective costumes and in them the symbolic value of the color red mingles with the health-protecting magic of the coral-color. Artificial corals and red beads were equally coveted in certain areas of Africa and they were given such eloquent designations as "kiswaili kimara pamba" - which signifies that the buyer was ready to ruin himself for them - or "kifouga mji" - which means they turned the women's heads.[1]

In Europe as well as in Africa we can find plenty of other social signals expressed by colors and colored beads, sometimes in striking similarity. This is the case for the use of the color red but it also applies to the color blue: in Maasai society, blue is the color of the married woman just as it is in various European costumes.

[1]Farcy, 1985:551

A girl's costume from Bohemia, nineteenth/twentieth century. The abundance of red, including red beads and red buttons, says...I am not yet married...

A girl from Kenya with plenty of beaded strings around her neck. The red strings say...I am not yet married...and...I can already have children...

A costume doll from India, twentieth century. The beadwork is composed of Indian beads, fine red drawn beads, green wound beads and golden blown beads.

Three necklaces with "coral" beads, Gablonz and Neugablonz, twentieth century. Red glass beads meant social signals yet they were also appreciated for their close resemblance to natural corals which since ancient times have been esteemed for their magical value. The upper necklace is a fashionable "Art Deco" necklace from Gablonz, 1930s, and the two-stranded necklace is a "coral" necklace from 1950s Neugablonz. It pretends to be a genuine coral necklace. The middle necklace from Gablonz, early twentieth century, is composed of interlocking toggles. These were standard Bohemian "coral" beads for the African trade.

The costume of a young bride from Bohemia, nineteenth/twentieth century. The color red dominates until marriage, while the married woman will change to costumes where the color blue is dominant.

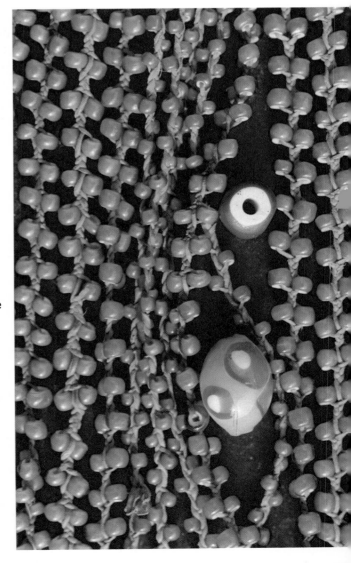

A lady with her dress abundantly decorated with black beads, Germany, 1868. In those years the black beads might still have a symbolic/social meaning, indicating mourning yet the fashionable use of black beads started in the nineteenth century.

Venetian "coral" beads for the African trade, twentieth century. Such overlay beads were the typical variety of artificial corals from Murano/Venice, yet such red overlay beads were made in other European countries as well. The large oval bead is a studio bead from Murano, 1989. It includes small overlay beads.

A costume doll from Poland, twentieth century. The red vest decorated with beads indicates that this is the costume of an unmarried girl.

A costume doll from Southern Africa, twentieth century.

A European bride with abundant pearl ornaments. Pearls on bridal costumes are mainly the symbols of purity.

A costume doll from Hungary, twentieth century. The abundance of red on the costume and the red beadwork on the cap says...I am not yet married...

## Loving beads

Another variety of beads with social symbolism is found both in Africa, as well as in Europe.

Zulu beadwork includes the so-called love-letters made by girls for the young man with whom they are in love. The bead-language found in these letters is almost as sophisticated as a kind of secret code.

*While colours have different symbolic meanings, these vary according to the area, and the relationship of colours within the 'letter' can modify or reinforce the colour meaning. The colours mostly used are white, black, red, pink, yellow, green and blue. White is the commonest and equals purity and truth. Black may represent the black skirt worn at marriage, or disappointment and mourning. Red can mean the fires of passionate love, or blood, anger and pain. Pink is a symbol of royalty since Mpande, a former Zulu king, adopted pink beads as his own; they may also mean poverty and a vow. Yellow, in its positive meaning, stands for pumpkins, and therefore a home and wealth; negatively it means calf dung and is a term of abuse. Green is grass and thus fields and a homestead, domestic bliss or that the sender is pining away. Blue comes in different shades, pale, royal and navy blue, and may mean loving fidelity, a request, sky, sea or talkative gossip. Blue and white striped beads represent the striped locusts that cling together when mating and "stay together for life.*[1]

In 19th century Europe we can find similar beadwork, but the European "love-letters" are less eloquent and easily decipherable. European girls used to please the young man of their fancy for example with beadwork including a sequence of flowers whose initials formed the girls name. A pansy in the beadwork was meant to say "think of me" or "I think of you" and the dominance of the blue color - the color of the forget-me-nots - wanted to say about the same thing. The roses and the red color stood for love and a snake encircling the flowers meant "eternal love."

[1]Carey, 1986:55/56

A beaded tobacco bag from Germany, nineteenth century. The bag is decorated with elaborate roses and forget-me-nots. It was made as a token of love.

Beaded purse and long necklace from Germany, nineteenth century. Both beadworks include plenty of roses, the flower which used to signal "love."

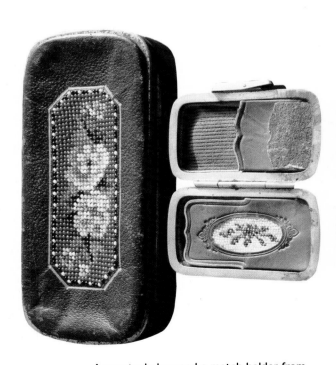

A spectacle box and a match holder from Germany, nineteenth century. These are other typical tokens made by German girls for their fiancés. The beadwork once again includes roses, saying "I love you."

Zulu "love-letter" from South Africa, twentieth century.

## Striking Beads

In old societies - whether European or African - the headgear played a "prominent" role providing social information, and was closely followed by all the upper parts of the body, thus we find sophisticated beadwork in those upper areas more than anywhere else.

Important headgear originally expressed high social ranking - such as a king's crown, a bishop's tiara, or a doctor's hat. In African as well as in European costumes, we find wonderfully beaded headgears.

A beaded chest ornament of a bridal costume from Germany, early twentieth century. The ornament includes blown and lined beads and tiny mirrors to deflect the evil eye.

A bridal head ornament from Bohemia, nineteenth/twentieth century. The ornament is composed of blown and lined beads.

An abundantly beaded cap which is part of a costume from Germany, nineteenth/twentieth century.

A bridal crown from the Black Forest/Germany, circa 1825 (Franziskaner Museum Villingen-Schwenningen). Similar bridal crowns were customary throughout the various German regions. The crown is decorated with plenty of blown and lined beads and with little mirrors to deflect the evil eye.

An Egyptian beaded collar from the period of Amenophis II. Such striking beaded collars were an indispensable part of the costume for every high ranking Egyptian from the period of the Old Kingdom until the end of the Egyptian Empire. The additional amulet string, the bangle bracelets, the earrings...every element of this Egyptian jewelry closely resembles African ornaments.

German woodcut of the 16th century depicting a bride from Danzig (Gdansk/Poland) with a heavily beaded ornament on the head and a rosary.

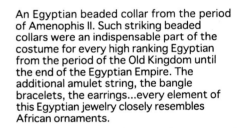

A costume cap from Frankonia/Germany, 19th century. The cap is ornamented all over with MOP bugles and it looks like it is made of brilliant silver.

Sketch of the striking beaded ornaments worn by the Benin king (Nigeria) when the first Europeans met him in the 16th century. Such heavy multi-stranded beaded neck ornaments were a customary royal ornament since antiquity - as we know it from the terracotta finds of the Nok-period.

Eye-catching disc necklets from Kenya, nineteenth/twentieth century. Such disc necklets are part of the Maasai costume.

A Maasai necklet from Kenya, twentieth century. Similar necklets are presently made for tourists.

King Kazembe from Inner Africa as Antonio Gamitto had seen him in 1831/32: "His head was ornamented with a kind of mitre, pyramidal in shape and two spans high, made of brilliant scarlet feathers; round his forehead was a dazzling diadem of beads of various kinds and colours...neck and shoulders were covered with a kind of capuchin the upper part of which was covered with upturned cowries; there followed a band of pretty imitation jewels made of glass... the arm from elbow to wrist was decorated with a string of bright blue beads" (Cunnison, 1960).

Hairdo from Inner Africa, early twentieth century. The ornament is composed of cylindrical beads in the colors blue and red and of white cowrie shells.

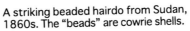

A man's headdress of the Dinka from Sudan, 1860s. "The Dinka have like quite a few Africans only poor hair and thus they like to wear caps and other headgears. Near of Kudj I saw frequently those strange caps which were exclusively composed of the large cylindrical beads which they name "Muria" in Chartoum" (Schweinfurth, 1922:79).

A striking beaded hairdo from Sudan, 1860s. The "beads" are cowrie shells.

Hairdo from Inner Africa, early twentieth century. The imaginative arrangement of the hair is accentuated by rows of white cylindrical beads.

## Fashionable Beads

In modern times glass beads are generally used "just for fun" with sometimes only a faint reminescence of the meaningful use in past times.

Beaded hairdo from Germany, 1994. Among young people the colors of the beads might have a special meaning yet generally such a beaded hairdo is a fashion that lasts but a season.

Egyptian fashions in the period of the 11th dynasty including a network of bugles. Almost identical beadwork fashions reappeared again in medieval Benin/Nigeria.

A stage costume which is abundantly decorated with black beads, Leipzig, 1910. Black beadwork on black dresses frequently had a social meaning in past times it indicating "mourning," yet black beads were among the cheapest beads and thus they were ideal elements for abundant fashionable ornaments.

The 1993 reinterpretation of the ancient beaded network fashions. This network is composed of amber-colored glass beads.

Beaded hairdo from Africa, modern. These beads might have a social significance yet in Africa beads were also used "just for fun" as soon as they became available in the late nineteenth century.

The beaded hairdo of a fashionable bride from Germany in 1994. Similar hairdos are known from ancient Egypt and from Africa.

German summer fashions in 1993. The dress is ornamented with a beaded belt which is composed according to traditional patterns of South American beadwork.

Beaded beard fashions from West Africa, 1914. This must have been a quite popular fashion as the German explorer Nachtigal reported in 1870 about an African chief in Sudan: "He asked me for some fashionable yet rare beads to adorn his beard. It took a long time until he was satisfied as most of the beads which I offered him didn't please him" (Nachtigal, 1879: 210).

Fashionable "pearls" from Neugablonz, 1950s, in front of German "pearl" fashions in 1994. In modern times "pearl" jewelry doesn't pretend to be genuine anymore but looks openly false in its eye-catching abundance.

German summer fashions in 1994 including fanciful "amulet" strings and three strings including millefiori beads from Murano, 1980s, and a string with a head pendant and two glassbeads from Java, modern. Similar necklaces became fashionable in Europe for the first time in the early 1970s and this exotic fashion has its repeated revival.

A necklace including Muranese beads, shell beads, malachite beads, silver beads and vertebra beads, Africa, uncertain period. Such necklaces are sold in Africa to the tourists. They generally include a mixture of old and modern beads. The Muranese beads on this necklace date back to approximately the first third of the twentieth century.

A necklace from India, modern. It includes among other beads and pendants some millefiori beads "in the Venetian manner." Such necklaces are frequently integrated into European summer fashions.

Six eye beads from Gablonz, late nine-teenth century. These are uncommonly well done eye beads achieved with underlaid foil and completed by a cobalt-blue pupil.

Five eye beads from Murano/Venice, twentieth century. This is a typical trade bead with an abstracted version of the eye pattern.

## Magic Beads

In modern times we wear beads and jewelry "just for fun." In the past, beads and similar ornaments often had a magic meaning. The social and the magic meaning were usually closely interwoven, thus the heavy beaded necklaces in ancient Egypt were not only meant to show the high rank of its wearer, but also to protect him. This protective magic of the royal ornaments was even imported into medieval Europe - as well via Byzantium as via old Jewish traditions.

### Eye beads

Every type of bead used to have its particular magic qualities - either from its shape or its material, or from its color which stood for certain materials. The "eye-beads" are possibly the best known magical beads. Those "dotted" beads are but one expression of a most ancient magic linked to the belief in the power of eye contact, to which a benevolent power was sometimes attributed, but more often a malevolent force was. We are still far from fully understanding the eye magic and its manifold symbols - but the eye-bead and the mirror-ornament are easily understandable: both are meant to deflect the evil eye. The oldest known eye-beads made from glass date approximately from the 15th-13th century BC. In the Egyptian bead industries of that period, these beads seem to have been the dominant type and they appeared in a great variety of fancy designs; while the Mesopotamian eye-beads were less sophisticated and apparently did not have the same importance for the bead industry. The early beads have usually only one or very few eyes achieved with inlaid glass drops or rings impressed into the bead core. Since the 7th century the patterns and techniques diversified:

- On multilayered eye-beads the design was built up from glass drops overlaying each other. Eventually the eye was additionally ground to reveal the various layers in contrasting colors.

- By the 5th century BC mosaic eye-beads began to appear. They included cane sections, each showing an eye design. Since the 3rd century BC this technique seems to have largely replaced the layered technique in the Mediterranean.[1]

Glass eye-beads are still made in Europe, but they have never again been made to such perfection as they were in antiquity. A main reason for this is that the European bead industries paid more attention to other sorts of "magic" beads starting in the Middle Ages.

[1]Spaer, 1985: 3

Several eye beads from Ghana, modern. These beads are made from powdered glass.

An amulet string from Ethiopia, nineteenth/
twentieth century. Most of the beads on this
string are from Murano/Venice, nineteenth/
twentieth century and some beads are
from Gablonz, nineteenth century.

An African singer in the 1860s with many
amulet strings.

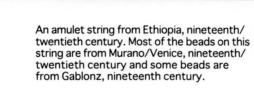

A marriage headgear from Southern
Germany, nineteenth/twentieth century.
The many mirrors are meant to deflect the
evil eye.

Yoruba beadwork from West Africa,
nineteenth/twentieth century. The Ibeji
religion involves the worship of human twins.

Yoruba beadwork from West Africa, nineteenth/twentieth century. The Yoruba believe that twins are two bodies sharing a single soul.

An important "Fastnacht" headgear from Austria, nineteenth/twentieth century, including glass beads and mirrors. Such costumes are worn at traditional celebrations which are meant to chase away the (winter) demons. Such celebrations take place in Southern Germany, Austria, and Switzerland.

A baby with the habitual string of corals around the neck, Germany, 1897. The corals were meant to conjure health.

A portrait of a man holding a man's rosary, Germany, 1578.

Natus Berlini Aō
1510. flor. adhuc
Aō 1578.

## Paternoster (=rosary) beads

The magic of repeated prayers is recorded in Christian belief since the 4th century AD. Towards the 11th century such prayer sequences became institutionalized as a prayer aid for the Christian laity unable to participate in the sophisticated Latin rituals. As the Pater Noster was the popular prayer it became the rudiment of the repetitions, which were not yet necessarily connected to a prayer string. But apparently by the 13th century it had already become a habit to wear a rosary among the clergy and the upper classes.[1]

The most important changes in this field occurred in the 14th/15th century. Medieval structures had begun to crumble in the 14th century when the abuse of power within the church led to the Schism (1376-1417) with several popes opposing each other. This deep crisis affected the entire church. A unifying symbol was urgently needed - and was found in the rosary-prayer which allowed every Christian his own independent practice of piety, at the same time uniting the community of Christians. This new praying system was perfected during the 15th century by the

Benedictines and the Dominicans, brotherhoods which contributed largely to the spreading of this praying mode. By the end of the 15th century it was considered to be the most attractive way of praying and had affected the entire population so deeply "that one might call it almost a mass psychosis."[2]

Christian prayer-counting had started with two different instruments - a string of beads including a free number of beads, and the prayer-"crown" with a limited number of beads. The crown existed in an open and a closed version. The short open crown became the prayer string for men - which led to the designation "cavaliersbetten" (=men's praying). The closed crown existed in three versions until the end of the 15th century:

- Short - comprising 10 - 25 beads,
- Medium - with 26 - 50 beads,
- Large - named Psalter or Chapelet - including 150 beads. It was almost exclusively worn by women and generally worn as a necklace.

This praying system was modified over and over again. Around 1600 the sequence of prayers had reached the actually valid form. Until the 17th century, a medal was used as the final pendant. In the 18th century, it was replaced by the crucifix - which led to the dropping of the credo cross in the 19th century.

The rosary beads were made by the "paternoster" makers. Corresponding guilds are recorded in Paris and Lübeck, for example, since the last third of the 13th century. Many organic materials were used for making rosary beads, most of them were chosen for their magical powers! Glass beads began to be used about the 13th/14th century but only in the 18th century did they become the dominant rosary beads.

The function of the rosary as a counting tool was only of minor importance for many centuries. Far more important were its other aspects, including the fact that it was the leading amulet string for the Europeans! Magical powers were attributed to the single beads - depending on their material - and the rosary was also abundantly hung with further amulets. Although the rosary was meant to be a symbol of Christian devotion, it was transformed by popular practice into a pagan magical string. The European rosary was also a badge of respectability - and it was the only piece of jewelry which escaped the rigid costume laws. This led to continual excesses, and the rosary soon became an ongoing subject of controversy.

[1] Herbst, 1925:63
[2] Ritz, 1955:33

A German woodcut of the 16th century depicting a bride from Cologne with her rosary. This rosary is very long and elaborate and it is apparently a piece of jewelry.

A German woodcut of the 16th century depicting a respectable woman from Lithuania with her rosary. Rosaries were not only ornaments but also badges of respectability.

Two rosaries with garnet-colored beads, Austria, twentieth century. The beads are from Gablonz. These are very common rosaries.

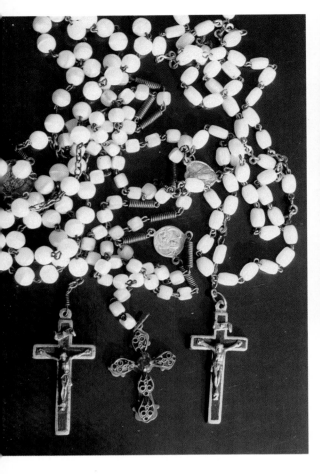

A silver rosary including garnet-colored beads, Southern Germany, nineteenth century. The beads are from Bavaria or Bohemia. This is an elaborate rosary with better glass beads and fine silver filigree work.

Three rosaries including white satin glass beads, Germany, twentieth century. The beads are from Gablonz.

Witches holding a counterfeit rosary, Germany, early 16th century. Such pictures indicate the link between amulet strings and rosaries.

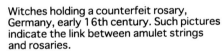

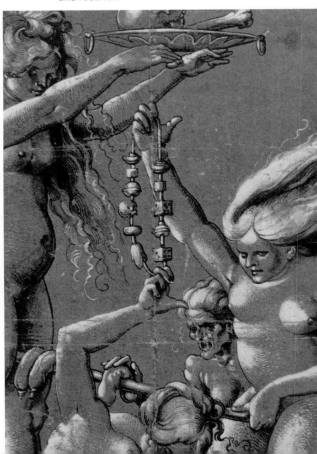

A silver rosary, uncertain origin, early twentieth century. The beads come from Gablonz. They show an abstracted eye pattern which is achieved with foil inlays. In the past rosaries were meant to protect the wearer and thus they included either magical pendants or at least magical beads.

A "Frais" (=disaster) string from Austria, 17th/
eighteenth century. Such amulet strings
were meant to protect against disaster.
And a rosary from Southern Germany, 16th/
17th century. The link between rosaries and
amulet strings was once extremely close.

A wooden rosary and a wooden prayer
string. Early rosary beads were rather cut
from organic materials. Glassbeads
became the dominant rosary beads only in
the eighteenth century.

## Head beads

The striking head beads which appeared for the first time around 700
BC are presumably the vitreous version of the magic head pendants previously made from metal or terracotta. The function of such head pendants was
doublefold: in certain civilizations they were symbols of slain enemies, but
they were also an elaborate version of the eye-bead. They were eventually
created to overrule other producers of more standard eye-beads - as they
came upon the market when eye-beads were again in high demand. The
inspiration for such vitreous head pendants might have come from Africa;
these beads were apparently mainly produced in Carthage. The many
Carthaginian industries were linked to the various demands of the African
market more than any other Phoenician industries - especially as the precious raw materials from Africa were so important for Phoenician trade.
Metallic versions of similar head pendants are (later) found in various civilizations but are specifically abundant in Africa. Other possible inspirators might
have been the Celts who also had close trading links with the Carthaginians,
and head pendants occur just as frequently in their ornaments. A considerable amount of head beads have been found in the area of ancient Etruria -
but there is no further artistic or cultural evidence that the Etruscans inspired
this bead design. As the Phoenician and the Etruscans were political allies for
quite a while, with an important trade connection, the attractive beads could
have arrived there for no reason other than this alliance.

Sketch of a terracotta head pendant from
Nigeria, Nok-period, circa 500 BC - 200 AD.
(The pendant is in the collection of the
National Museum Lagos, Nigeria)

A head bead from glass artist Cristiano Balbi in Venice. 1993. In the background is visible a Phoenician headbead, circa 500 BC.

Two "head" beads from Gablonz, 1920s. Such head beads had been created in the 1920s. "Egyptian" design became fashionable when the tomb of Tutenkhamun had been discovered.

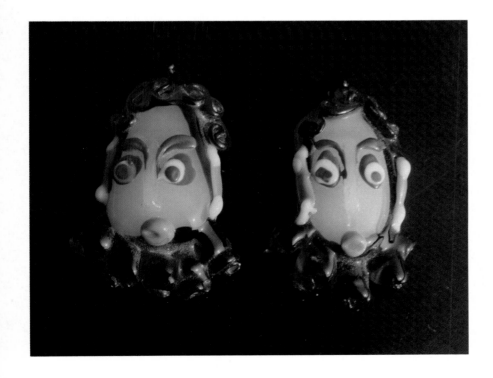

Two head beads made by L. A. V. Cooperativa from Murano, 1993.

Several head beads from Murano/Venice.
Such modern interpretations of the old
theme have no link to any head bead
magic.

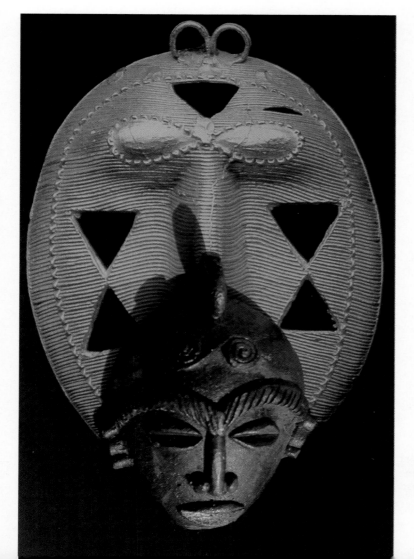

A Naga with a head amulet, Nagaland,
North-East India, 1930s.

A head amulet from the Ivory Coast,
modern, in front of a wonderfully stylized
golden head amulet from the Ivory Coast,
nineteenth century.

A bead including twenty-three portrait canes, Purdalpur, North India, modern. The Indian lampworkers are presently making a large range of beads "in the Venetian manner."

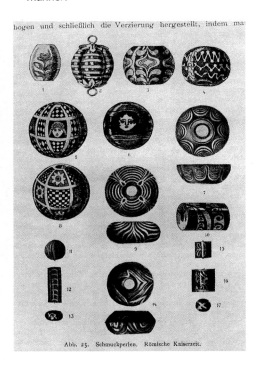

## Portrait beads

The antique beadmakers created another facial bead which intrigued European archaeologists and beadmakers more than any other and was recreated on repeated occasions until present time. Those beads were, technically speaking, mosaic beads in which one or several canes showed a human face. The Egyptian beadmakers created these beads for the first time around the 2nd/1st century BC.

Such face canes were inserted into many types of beads ranging from simple to elaborate beads. The most elaborate versions of such portrait beads feature detailed face canes alternating with other motifs, such as checker fields or stars. The beads are quite large, measuring generally 2.5 cm in diameter. They have been found in contexts attributable to the late Roman period (400-600 AD). Most of them were found in Scandinavia, and some in Poland, Northern Hungary, and in Southern Germany. Archaeologists have written about these beads for seventy years, trying to unriddle their meaning and their origin. Recently, it was suggested that the beads depict Constantine the Great and that they were imperial gifts to important Germanic representatives. The likely production places have been suggested as the two capitals in Constantine's early reign; i.e., either Rome or Trier.[1]

These antique portrait beads had at least a symbolic meaning if not also a magic power but when such elaborate beads were recreated for the first time in the 1840s by Jacopo Franchini in Venice, it was done for the technical challenge.

[1]Stout, 1991:107

*Left:*
Various antique beads including two portrait beads. The right portrait bead is attributed to 100 BC - 100 AD and the left bead is attributed to 400 - 600 AD.

Some portrait canes of glass artist Jacopo Franchini from Venice, mid-nineteenth century (Glass Museum Murano). The Franchinis made most elaborate millefiori and portrait canes yet their canes are rarely found in beads. Instead they were included into fashionable items for the European market such as flat jewelry elements which were mounted in gold.

Nine very elaborate portrait beads of an unknown maker from Murano/Venice, second half of the nineteenth century (Courtesy G. Sarpellon).

# SOME HIGHLIGHTS OF BEAD TECHNOLOGY AND BEAD ART

## *Foiled beads*

In foiled beads, a thin layer of metallic foil - mostly silver or gold - is included between layers of glass. Such beads have the splendor of the precious metal but little of the expensive material is required, and sandwiched in between the vitreous layers it will neither wear off nor tarnish as happens when gold or silver is only applied to the surface of the glass.

Foil inclusion into glass is a difficult technique that dates back to antiquity. To our knowledge, the oldest such gold-glass was made during the Hellenistic period - around the 3rd century BC - mainly in Alexandria and on the island of Rhodes, where a major production site for glass (beads) was established around the late 3rd/early 2nd century BC. Various excavations, such as the workshop of Phidias in Olympia from the 5th century BC and Phoenician ivories dating from the 9th/8th century BC - where the experts discovered inlays from transparent glass backed by thin gold foil - reveal that this design and technique had its roots in Phoenician crafts.

The technique knew its greatest success in Byzantine mosaics and beads. It was brought from the Byzantine workshops - most likely by Benedictine monks - to the Rhineland workshops where such beads were also made. With the fall of the Byzantine Empire, the Venetians became the main producers of foiled glass, first applying this craft to mosaic glass. The craftsmen of the "Serenissima" perfected this technique and in the 16th century also applied it to small items such as knife handles, [1] but probably not yet to beads. Instead we can learn from documentary sources that in the late 18th century they produced the same varieties of "metallic" beads as their strongest competitors in Bavaria/Bohemia/Thuringia - such as "silver"-lined beads and gold-coated beads. During the 19th century, the Muranese/Venetians, as well as the Bohemians, once again took up the old technique of casing the metallic leaf in between glass to make it indestructible for their beads. Presently, the Japanese craftsmen are the most competent competitors of the Europeans in this field.

[1]Zecchin I, 1987:264

A three-stranded necklace including foil beads, Murano/Venice, 1960s. This is a fashionable version of foil beads. The traditional Venetian foil beads have the entire core covered with foil.

A necklace composed of flat foil beads, Murano/Venice, 1930s. Spatters of colored glass had been applied upon the foil and were additionally encased by irregularily applied clear glass. This is a very unusual version of foil beads.

A necklace composed of cobalt blue
beads including a star-shaped foil
decoration, Gablonz, 1920s/30s. This is an
extremely rare version of foil beads.

A multistranded necklace from Murano/
Venice, 1993. The design had been made
by Lanvin/France in circa 1984.

A necklace composed of silver foil beads,
designed by Butler & Wilson, 1993. The
beads are from Murano.

Close-up of the previous necklace: these
beads represent the modern version of foil
beads. The foil is covered by irregularily
applied colored glass and some beads
have a matte finish. The special attraction
of this necklace lies in its overall design and
the well matching colors of the beads.

Two necklaces including gold coated beads on which the gold foil has only partly been covered by clear glass trailings. The beads on the central strands are from Murano/Venice, 1920s, and the beads on the two outer strands had been made by the E. Moretti & f.lli company, 1994. The modern and the older golden beads are equally attractive yet the older beads are covered by far more trailings. More trailings mean more time-consuming work.

A necklace including various types of foil beads as well as gold coated beads, Murano, 1992.

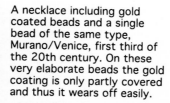

A necklace including gold coated beads and a single bead of the same type, Murano/Venice, first third of the 20th century. On these very elaborate beads the gold coating is only partly covered and thus it wears off easily.

A necklace including foil beads and iridescent beads, uncertain origin, 1950s. These are very uncommon and elaborate beads: they are foiled, pinched, and have a luster finish.

A sample card with "fiorate" (=flowered) beads from Murano/Venice, nineteenth century (Glass Museum Murano). These beads are extremely elaborate and specifically the roses are designed with unequalled care.

## Flower beads

Lampworked beads with flower-like decorations were made by Muranese/Venetian lampworkers since at least the last third of the 18th century. The manufacturers/merchants Acquabona, Barbaria, and Giacomuzzi offered such beads in this period.[1] A reference in 1762 from James Bruce saying "He had bought us a quantity (of beads) beautifully flowered with red and green" could refer to such beads as well.[2] The earliest such beads which are exactly dated are found on the Barbaria sample card of 1815. This sample card includes various types of "fiorate" (=flowered) beads but not yet the "Biedermeier" variety decorated with "roses" and "forget-me-nots" - the design which became the standard. It is very possible that this romantic design was created in the first half of the 19th century to satisfy the European taste for flower symbolism. We don't know whether they were well accepted on the European market, as the Muranese/Venetian craftsmanship was only duly recognized in Europe after the Viennese exhibition in 1845 and as the "fashionable" Europeans were generally less interested in the new and imaginative design lines from the Italian glassmakers but rather in their copies of antique glass. Yet it seems as if those wonderful beads were a great success at least in the second half of the 19th century. The Gablonz craftsmen began to create such buttons and beads as well in this period - and it is generally a clear sign of a market success when a competitor takes up the same design line. It is undeniable that the Bohemians got their inspiration from the Italian beads, yet their flower beads are different enough to be appreciated as an independent variation on the same theme. As the elaborate beads were created in Murano/Venice as well as in Bohemia by cottage workers, it is impossible to find out when exactly they were made for the first time in the Gablonz area. A sample card of the export company Mahla confirms that such buttons were exported since at least the last third of the 19th century. This design line has never been discontinued.

[1]Zecchin I, 1987:92+94+189
[2]Hibbert, 1982:29

A necklace including blue biconical beads with flower-like decorations, Murano/Venice, nineteenth century. This type of "flower" pattern had been designed at least as early as the late eighteenth century.

A sample card with "fiorate" beads from Murano/Venice, nineteenth century (Glass Museum Murano). These round beads are again very elaborate.

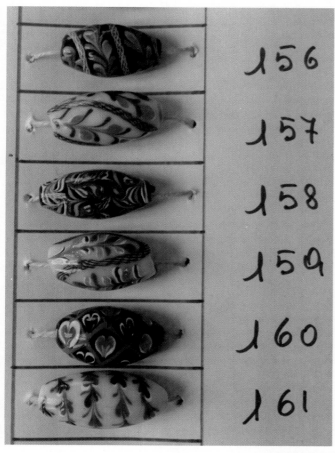

156

157

158

159

160

161

A necklace including a very fine modern variety of flower beads, Murano, 1992. These beads compare well to the old beads and they represent an uncommon variety among the modern beads.

A sample card including lampworked beads with a flowerlike design, Murano/Venice, nineteenth century (Glass Museum Murano). The beads are again exceptionally elaborate. Many of the beads in the museum's collection were given directly by the manufacturers to the museum and this explains why they are so very well done.

Close-up of a necklace including very large and very elaborate flower beads, Murano/Venice, nineteenth century. The large beads have a diameter of 2.3 centimeters.

A necklace including some flower beads, Gablonz, 1930s. These are quite uncommon Bohemian flower beads - first because of their design and second because the flowers are not marvered into the bead core.

Flower beads on three necklaces from Murano/Venice, twentieth century. The light-blue beads which are combined to golden beads are quite elaborate, while the other beads are standard ones.

Lampworked flower beads on two necklaces from Murano/Venice, 1920s. A very typical feature of the 1920s is the yellowish shade of the green "leafs" on the beads.

A necklace of the previous picture revealing the length of it. The original length of such necklaces lies generally around 100 centimeters.

A lady wearing a necklace with large glass beads, Germany 1919. The picture shows the standard length of such necklaces.

A necklace including flower beads, Gablonz, 1920s/30s. The "flowers" are framed with delicate aventurine trailings.

Three flower beads on a similar necklace as the previous one, Gablonz, 1920s/30s. In Gablonz, the flowers were mostly worked upon satin glass and yellow satin glass was apparently the most frequently chosen shade.

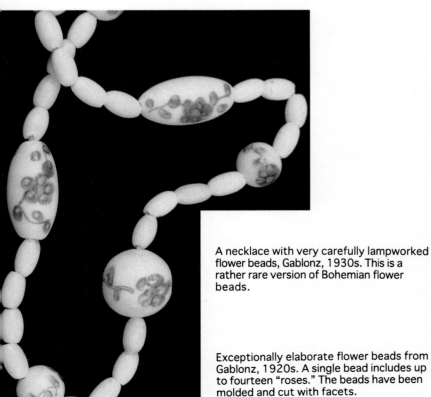

A necklace with very carefully lampworked flower beads, Gablonz, 1930s. This is a rather rare version of Bohemian flower beads.

Exceptionally elaborate flower beads from Gablonz, 1920s. A single bead includes up to fourteen "roses." The beads have been molded and cut with facets.

Flower beads on a blue necklace from
Gablonz, 1920s/30s. The glass of the
beadcore is again satin glass.

An elaborate flower bead on a necklace
from Gablonz, 1920s. Two shades of satin
glass are combined in this bead and the
flower is also covered with crystal.

Five flower beads which had been created
by Rudolf Waller in the 1950s. R. Waller
originated from Seidenschwanz near
Gablonz and after the expulsion from
Bohemia he settled in Neugablonz.
Lampworking such beads had been a
family tradition.

A necklace including flower beads, possibly from Jablonec, 1950s.

A close-up of the previous necklace revealing the net-inlay underneath the lampworked flowers. Such net-inlay had been a 1950s design line of the Harrachov glassworks near Jablonec.

## Mosaic beads

Mosaic beads were created around 1500 BC. Technically speaking, they are made by marvering multicolored cane slices into a bead core, or by combining cane segments into a bead. As those cane segments frequently display a flower-like pattern, the term "millefiori" (=thousand flowers) was introduced in the 19th century to describe glass items done in this technique.

Such mosaic beads (and mosaic vessels) were obviously again a great success in Hellenistic and Roman periods as they were made abundantly in the period between 300 BC and 400 AD, especially in Alexandrian workshops. Later they were also made elsewhere, such as in the Rhineland, around 500/600 AD. In the eastern Mediterranean the design had an important revival around 900 AD, and was finally re-discovered and re-created in 15th/16th century Murano in the famous glass "a rosete." Mosaic glass had its ultimate rediscovery in the European glass industries in the first half of the 19th century. Various famous glassworks produced it for a very short while until it again became the sole privilege of the Muranese to create this elaborate glass.

Mosaic beads were apparently only made on larger scale towards the late 19th century. In the beginning they were meant for African trade yet in the 20th century they were also made for the European market. Since the early 20th century the finest mosaic beads have been created by the Ercole Moretti & f.lli company in Murano. This company was established in 1911 for the production of the classical Rosetta bead and millefiori mosaics. They recreated standard mosaic beads and have designed entirely new versions of this classical theme to this day.

A necklace including millefiori beads from Murano, modern. The beads are similar yet not identical to the beads in the next picture. The metal beads and the metal pendant are from Africa. Such necklaces are sold in Africa to the tourists.

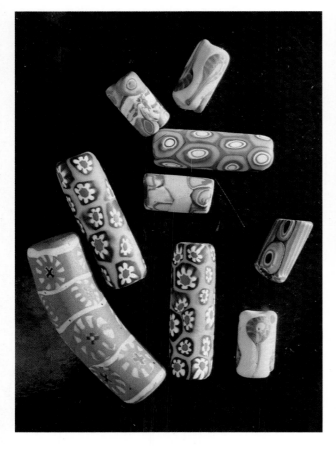

Two mosaic glass plates from the E. Moretti & f.lli company, Murano, 1982, designed by Gianni Moretti (Courtesy G. Moretti). As regards mosaic glass the Europeans had always a rather conventional taste. They liked the mosaic glass vessels which reproduced antique design best and had some difficulty in accepting fine modern mosaic design.

Millefiori beads from the E. Moretti & f.lli company of Murano, twentieth century.

Three little vases from the Fratelli Toso company of Murano, 1920s. Since the mid-nineteenth century, the Europeans had appreciated the mosaic glass vessels while similar beads became only fashionable on the European market since about the 1920s. Such little vases which reproduce antique design lines became a real craze in the early twentieth century.

Two necklaces including cylindrical millefiori beads from Murano, 1920s/30s. The beads on the right side have a matte finish. Such cylindrical beads are the typical beads of the African trade - yet here they have been strung with glass (at left) and wooden (at right) beads from Gablonz and these necklaces were clearly meant for the European market. Each necklace is nearly 100 centimeters long and has a tassel.

Two necklaces with millefiori beads from Murano and wooden beads from Gablonz, 1920s/30s. The millefiori beads of the outer necklace had already been included in the previous picture. The stringing pattern as well as the types of the accompanying beads are sometimes very helpful as the age of millefiori beads is not always easily determined.

A necklace with millefiori beads from Murano, 1930s. These beads include quite unusual cane segments with aventurine and white filigree. They are best seen on the large bead in the middle. These are very fine Moretti canes which had been created in the 1920s and which help to decide about the age of the beads. Another such helpful cane segment is the black-and-white cane which is visible on four of the medium-sized beads. A new black-and-white cane has been created yet the modern cane has much thicker white layers and thus it is quite easy to recognize it.

A necklace with millefiori beads in various sizes, Murano, 1920s/40s. This necklace includes plenty of pre-war cane segments. The most characteristic feature on them are the many stripes on the outside of various canes.

Four necklaces including elaborate millefiori beads, Murano, 1920s. Except for the necklace with the dominantely blue beads, all beads are from the E. Moretti & f.lli company. These beads represent a very fashionable design line in millefiori beads. The design is very convincing as each bead is composed of a single cane type - instead of including a haphazard mixture of cane segments - and each bead has a perfect finish.

One necklace of the previous picture. The beads are strung in the typical pattern of the 1920s with a tassel at the end of the necklace.

Three necklaces with millefiori beads from Murano, 1920s/30s. Not only the cane segments can help to decide about the age of the beads, sometimes their shape can as well. The biconical and the square beads were "fashionable" beads of the 1920s/30s, which were created for the European market.

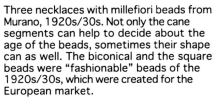

Lady wearing a long necklace with glass beads, Germany, 1930s.

Two necklaces including millefiori beads from Murano, 1920s. The beads have a very elaborate design which is typical of the 1920s.

A necklace with millefiori beads from Murano/Venice, uncertain period, possibly 1940s/50s. Again these are pinched beads yet each bead has only got three pinches.

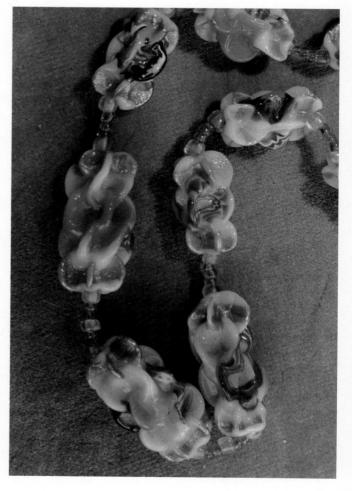

A necklace with millefiori beads from Murano/Venice, 1920s/40s. These beads required very time-consuming lampwork as each bead has fifteen to twenty-five pinches in addition to the inclusion of the cane segments.

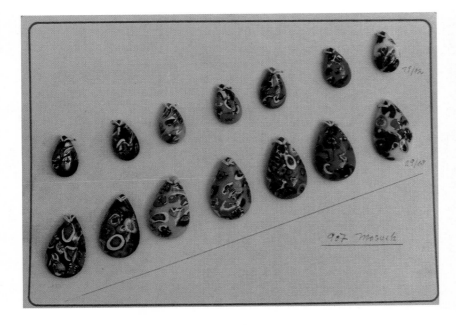

A sample card with millefiori beads from Wildner of Neugablonz, 1970s. The Gablonzers as well as the Neugablonzers also made millefiori beads yet on a much smaller scale then the lampworkers from Murano and Venice. They generally used cane segments from Murano but occasionally they made their own canes as well.

A long necklace including "turquoise" and "lapis" beads, Neugablonz, 1960s. The necklace has the fashionable length of the 1960s. The "turquoise" beads are additionally pinched to give them the appearance of the raw stone.

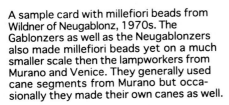

Two necklaces with millefiori beads. The necklace with the melon-shaped oblong beads is from Murano, 1920s/30s. The beads on the other necklace were possibly made in Neugablonz.

## Artificial Pearls and Beads

Glass beadmaking began in the Middle East with imitation beads - glass and fayence beads that looked like carnelian, turquoise, and lapis lazuli.

The earliest known Venetian beads were yellow - imitating amber.[1] The "crystal" beads of around 1500 were definitely made to resemble closely rock crystal beads.[2] Faceted "crystal" beads which were apparently made neither in Murano nor in Venice caused considerable turmoil in 1502 as their import and sale was considered a threat to the established and profitable Venetian production and trade of rock crystal beads.[3] The "cristalleri" in 1505 still had to guarantee that their crystal beads were genuine rock crystal beads.[4] The possibility of imitation also possibly became involved in 1585 when a newly perfected glass - suitable for drawing bead canes - was named after precious stones such as emerald and topaz,[5] and in 1700 when the red glass made by Orsella Mantovani, which was suitable for lampworked beads, was named "ruby."[6] The Muranese "calcedonio" beads, which appeared for the first time in written records in 1496,[7] were certainly meant to resemble natural stones as well. From Ximenes in Antwerp we learn of an early 17th century request from Africa for imitation beads resembling a rare natural stone (see page 73) and "coral" beads were apparently requested from African customers since at least about the 17th century, and until the 20th century they were reckoned among the most coveted beads in certain regions - which caused an almost unlimited variety of reproduction corals throughout the centuries.

The stupendous green of malachite: a silver rosary with malachite beads, a mirror backed with malachite glass from Gablonz, 1930s and a necklace with malachite glass beads, Gablonz, 1930s.

A "Rosequartz" necklace from Gablonz, nineteenth century. The large stone is molded with an intricate pattern to simulate carving. It is mounted in silver filigree and the necklace has the design of a traditional costume necklace of the nineteenth century. The stone and the beads are made from alabaster glass.

Close-up of three necklaces with green "stone" beads imitating malachite, chrysoprase, and tourmaline (from left to right). The glass beads are from Gablonz, 1930s. Such perfect "malachite" and "chrysoprase" beads have only been made in the 1930s. The tourmaline-type beads have been made since the early twentieth century until the present time.

A necklace with "marble" beads and "lapis" beads, possibly from Gablonz, 1930s. The background shows Egyptian amulets made of "lapis" glass, attributed to 1400 BC. The modern glass beads so closely resemble their respective stones that one is easily decieved.

Two necklaces including "stone" beads. The right necklace has been strung in France and the left one has been recently restrung. The beads are possibly from Gablonz, 1930s.

Six "banded agate" beads in front of five agate stones. The beads are from Quedlinburg/Germany, 1950s. The exceptionally naturalistic coloring of the beads required elaborate lampworking to mix the amethyst-colored glass and the white glass properly. The beads have been molded in addition with sort of carvings to give them an even more natural appearance. The making of these beads was very time-consuming.

Two necklaces including different "stone" beads. The upper necklace is from Gablonz, 1930s, and the lower necklace is from Neugablonz, 1950s.

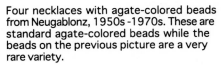

Four necklaces with agate-colored beads from Neugablonz, 1950s -1970s. These are standard agate-colored beads while the beads on the previous picture are a very rare variety.

Various necklaces with "lapis," "turquoise," "rosequartz," "amethyst," and "coral" beads from Neugablonz, 1950s/60s. Such necklaces were the standard complement to the equally standard woollen "twin-set" from England in the 1950s/60s.

A necklace including "coral"/"carnelian" beads from Murano/Venice, nineteenth/twentieth century. The glass beads are wound beads with a yellow core. Such beads were created to resemble coral beads and carnelian beads. Among American trade bead collectors they are named "cornaline d'Aleppo."

The fashionable way of wearing a solo "pearl" in 1914 Germany.

A Naga necklace from India with red overlay beads and white beads possibly from Murano, early twentieth century. Those small "coral" beads are drawn beads.

Two necklaces including fine baroque "pearls" from Gablonz, 1930s.

Artificial pearls - made from glass - were apparently on the market since about the second half of the 16th century. The sudden rise in demand for pearls and "pearls" was clearly caused by a fundamental change in European fashions which occurred around the 1650s.[8] Some of the oldest glass "pearls" are included in the collection of the Archiduke Ferdinand of Tyrol, dating back to the second half of the 16th century. Yet it seems as if other methods for making good looking and at least partly artificial pearls were investigated during the late 16th and the early 17th century with greater care than making glass "pearls" - such as molding large pearls from crushed small pearls. Even the famous Muranese glassmaker Giovanni Battista Darduin originally dealt with such pearl transformation[8], until towards the end of the 17th century he perfected the opalescent "girasole" which proved to be the most suitable glass for fine "pearls."

Artificial pearls in former times were mostly created from blown beads lined with a solution made from fish scales. Additionally, they were filled with wax to stabilize the lining as well as the entire bead. Presently, most "pearls" are made from massive glass beads which are covered with a pearly coating. Starting in the early 19th century we can find many references to such coated beads - named "Roman pearls." A German encyclopedia from 1834 differentiates between

- Roman pearls - which were made from (alabaster) glass with a wax coating.

- Artificial pearls - which were blown beads lined with "fish-silver" (the German term) or "essence d'orient" (the French term), both terms meaning the same solution of fish scales. The artificial pearls were made "above all in Rome, Florence, Venice, Vienna, and Paris."

- Glass beads - which were blown or drawn beads with colored or metallic lining.

This differentiation between Roman pearls and artificial pearls is found repeatedly throughout the 19th century in various European sources. The making of the finest "pearls" was quite often, if not to say dominantly, concentrated in and around the fashionable capitals. A well-known pearl-maker from Vienna was the lampworker Anton Schwefel - the glass artist who had decisively cooperated in the 1820s in making the first Austrian "incrustations." Such porcelain-like inclusions into glass are commonly named "sulphides" and they were a tremendous success on the fashionable European market in the 19th century.

Artificial pearls have remained a leading type of glass beads through the centuries. Up to the 20th century, most of them were blown beads, i.e. very fragile beads, and were mainly used to ornament dresses - making the request for them was almost unlimited.

[1]Zecchin III, 1990:15    [5]Zecchin II, 1989:167
[2]Zecchin I, 1987:236    [6]ibid.:63
[3]Cristalleri:45          [7]ibid.:212
[4]Gasparetto, 1958:185    [8]Zecchin I, 1987:173

Four fashionable "pearl" necklaces from Neugablonz, 1950s/60s. The fancy pattern on the upper necklace is a standard pattern on Neugablonz beads and the intricate stringing pattern of the lower necklace represents a typical design line of the 1950s.

The 1920s craze for pearls and "pearls."

Two necklaces and a bracelet with artificial pearls from Neugablonz, 1950s. Such dog-collar necklaces had been fashionable in the early twentieth century and had their revival in the 1950s.

Plenty of artificial pearls in a fabulous fashion jewelry brooch, modern. False pearls don't pretend to be the real thing anymore but come along in eye-catching overabundance.

A sample card with MOP beads from Murano/Venice, nineteenth century (Glass Museum Murano). Such lampworked beads which are composed of MOP canes in various colors are the most elaborate variety of MOP beads. The two broken beads reveal that these beads are hollow and thus very fragile. The oldest dated beads of this type are included in the Barbaria sample card of 1815 (see pages 59-62).

A beaded bag from Austria, early twentieth century. The beadwork includes silvery MOP beads. Their attractive sheen is well visible on this bag.

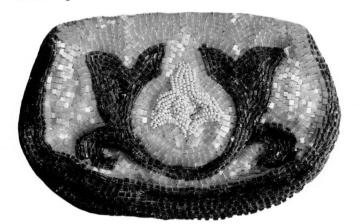

## Mother-of-Pearl (MOP) beads

MOP beads are always made from glass canes/tubes. They get their specific sheen from reflections within the glass. For this purpose the melt is generally made very bubbly, and when the glass is drawn into canes those bubbles are transformed into microscopic hollows. Sometimes the effect is also achieved by bundling tubes or even spun glass and redrawing the assembly. The MOP tubes are mostly cut into beads and bugles - yet they are eventually transformed into blown beads or used for the creation of elaborate lampworked beads.

MOP beads had possibly been "invented" as early as the 17th century[1], yet they appear in great abundance only in mid-18th century Rococo beadwork. Wherever they might have been created for the first time - in this period they were already being made in Russia, Bohemia, and Murano/Venice. They were an overwhelming success on the European market as they were a perfect substitute for silver embroidery work. The silver threads tarnished very quickly, while the MOP beads kept their silvery sheen forever. Because of this specific use, 18th century MOP beads were almost exclusively white beads. The beadmakers started apparently only in the first half of the 19th century to create further varieties in other colors. Such colored MOP beads were made in the early 19th century in Gablonz and in Murano/Venice. Written reference to such beads is found in various glass manuals since the 1840s. Best recorded is the involvement of Giovanni Battista Franchini in the perfection of MOP beads.[2] He concentrated on perfecting the rose colored variety (Madre perla rosea) and is said to have succeeded in this task in 1827.

The Muranese/Venetian lampworkers created throughout the 19th century unequalled lampworked beads from this glass. Such labor-intensive and fragile beads are not made anymore in modern times but simple drawn MOP beads and bugles are a standard variety until present time. They are mostly made in North Bohemia.

[1]Pazaurek, 1911:7
[2]Zanetti, 1867:18-21

A Russian icon decorated with MOP bugles, 19th century.

Rococo beadwork from Germany, eighteenth century. The beadwork is composed of MOP bugles. The silvery sheen of those beads was highly estimated for European beadwork.

Strands of drawn beads from Gablonz, early nineteenth century. These beads are equally MOP beads yet they don't include as many reflecting hollows as the previous beads and thus their sheen is less accentuated.

Two strands of blown beads from Gablonz, nineteenth/twentieth century. The four green beads are blown MOP beads. They were made from a thin tube which was only slightly inflated. This variety of MOP beads was made in the Gablonz area since the early nineteenth century.

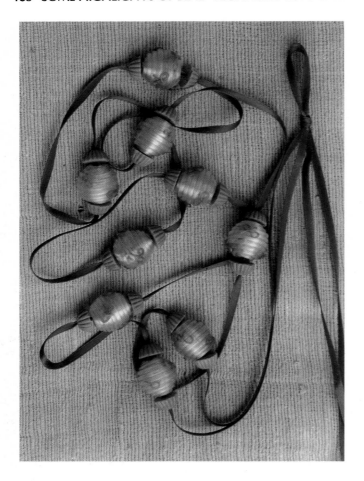

The English actress Lena Ashwell wearing a long necklace with similar MOP beads, England, 1905.

A long necklace with lampworked MOP beads, Murano, early twentieth century.

Close-up of four beads from the previous necklace. The beads are additionally decorated with lampworked applications.

A necklace including MOP beads from Murano/Venice, early twentieth century. These beads have very elaborate applications, including aventurine bows, flowers, and leaflets. The small beads are from Gablonz.

A necklace with silvery MOP beads and red-lined beads, Neugablonz, 1950s. The necklace is arranged upon a MOP glass vase from Bohemia, nineteenth century.

Three necklaces including elaborate satin glass beads, Gablonz, 1920s/30s. The designation "mother-of-pearl" is sometimes also applied to the Bohemian satin glass - yet the sheen of satin glass is achieved with different techniques. Generally the lampworker uses for satin glass special canes which include an opaque half and a transparent half.

An eye-catching necklace with satin glass beads, Neugablonz, 1950s. Satin glass beads were an overwhelming success on the market and the beads are still made in Bohemia as well as in Bavaria.

Various necklaces including MOP beads, Jablonec, 1950s-1970s. Such cylindrical beads with faceted ends in the shade blue and rose are the typical modern MOP beads.

Beadwork including metallic "bronze" beads, Germany, early twentieth century. These metal beads have still their attractive metallic brilliance but as such beads were made from iron they rusted easily.

A sample card with bronze beads from Murano/Venice, nineteenth century (Glass Museum Murano). The bronze coating has worn off on the larger beads and the dark core is visible. There is no technological necessity for taking a specific glasstype upon which the bronze or luster coating is applied. Generally the makers just took the cheapest varieties of glass to enhance them by those attractive coatings.

## Bronze Beads

"Metallic" glass beads reckoned among the most important bead varieties for the European market - in whatever technique they were created. The three shades gold, silver, and bronze/copper were the most required ones. Each of those "metal" beads was done with various techniques.

Bronze beads were introduced in the late 18th century. They must have been a great success on the European market and much consideration was given to such Venetian bronze beads in a German manual of 1849.

*There is a mysterious kind of beads in Venice. They have a copper-like surface and they along come in various shapes. The Italians take great care not to reveal how they are made. They are only slightly more expensive than the standard beads. The bead core is made from an opaque glass in a dark green shade. The seemingly metallic coating is extremely thin and very closely attached to the beads. The coating withstands acid solutions, yet disappears as soon as the beads are heated, and wears off after a while. The beads resemble closely a certain type of English earthenware.[1]*

We don't know for sure how the earliest Venetian bronze beads were made - yet apparently they were achieved in a similar way as luster coating. It is thought generally that the procedures to achieve such glass coatings were only introduced in the 1850s - but we know that many interesting techniques had in fact been developed by the beadmakers long before they became widely known, because they were successfully marketed on fashionable blown glass.

[1]Schreiber, 1849: 169 and 170

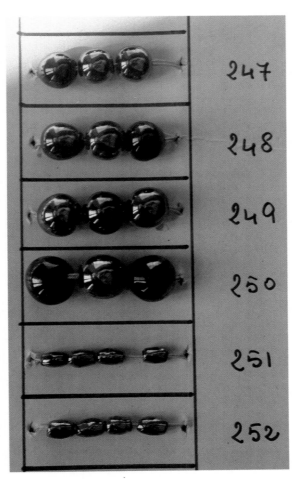

Bronze beads (and stones) on various pieces of fashion jewelry from Venice, Neugablonz and Jablonec, 1950s. The Bohemian makers specialized on faceted bronze beads while the typical Muranese variety were the small drawn beads on the second necklace from the top.

Necklaces including bronze beads, Venice, 1991. Bronze beads still remain a most appreciated variety of beads. They are presently very standard beads and yet are incorporated into such elaborate necklaces as seen on this picture.

Three necklaces including bronze beads. The necklace with the black and the bronze beads is from Venice, 1950s, and the two other necklaces are from Neugablonz, 1950s.

A necklace with very imaginative bronze beads, probably from Bohemia, uncertain period.

Plate in Carnival glass from the USA, twentieth century. The luster coating was an enormous success on the American market.

Three necklaces with luster beads, Neugablonz and Jablonec, 1950s. The vase from Bohemia, twentieth century is coated according to the same technique as the beads. Luster beads have a rainbow-like sheen yet the coating is applied in a similar way as the bronze coating.

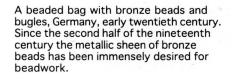

A beaded bag with bronze beads and bugles, Germany, early twentieth century. Since the second half of the nineteenth century the metallic sheen of bronze beads has been immensely desired for beadwork.

A necklace with faceted luster beads and a bracelet with faceted bronze beads, Neugablonz, 1950s. The metallic sheen of the luster coating is specifically eye-catching when it is applied upon black glass.

Three necklaces including luster beads, Warmensteinach/Bavaria, 1950s. The luster coating is identical yet the black beads are the most eye-catching variety. The beads on these necklaces have the standard shape of post-war pressmolded beads from Warmensteinach.

## Fancy and Fashionable Trailings

The trailing design is almost as old as glass and beadmaking itself. The decoration is, technically speaking, just as simple as can be yet it allows an incredible range of imaginative variations.

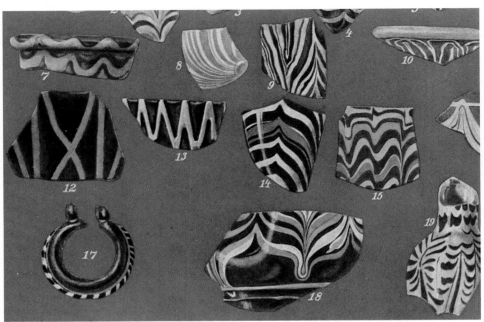

Egyptian glass fragments with trailed and pulled pattern, circa 14th century BC.

A strand of glass beads and organic beads. Some among them possibly date back to the 17th century. Such beads with two interlacing trailings, as on the black-and-white glass bead next to the green glass bead, had been made since antiquity.

Five turquoise colored beads with trailings, a gilded bead with red trailings and a button which is decorated in a similar way. The golden bead and the button are from Murano, twentieth century. The turquoise beads are from Gablonz, early twentieth century. Beads with such trailings are generally attributed to Murano/Venice yet the Bohemian lampworkers used this pattern as well.

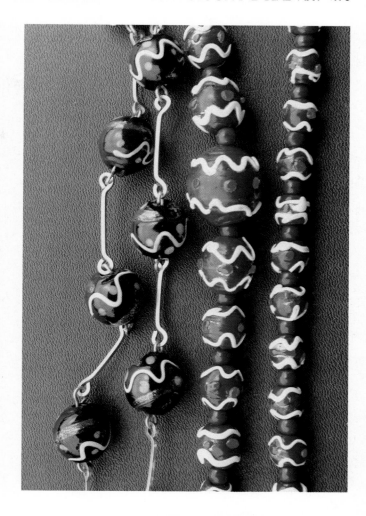

Three necklaces including beads with fancy trailings, Murano/Venice, late nineteenth/early twentieth century. All necklaces have been restrung with new spacers. Noteworthy is the overabundance in red trailings on the beads of the right strand. Whenever modern beads have this pattern, the amount of trailings is drastically reduced to finish the beads in shorter time. Noteworthy is as well the zig-zag pattern on the blue beads. This type of trailing pattern is rather rare.

Two necklaces with trailing patterns, Murano/Venice, twentieth century. The combination of trailings and dots is frequently found on beads for the African trade.

Two necklaces including beads with fancy trailings, Murano, 1970s (inner necklace) and 1992 (outer necklace). The pattern of the inner necklace was very time-consuming.

A sample card including beads with fancy trailings from Gablonz, 1930s/40s. (Museum Neugablonz) Most of the beads are additionally pinched into fancy shapes.

A sample card with lampworked beads from the Schuhmeyer workshop in Neugablonz, 1950s-70s. The sample card includes one row of beads with fancy trailings.

A black bead with pulled pattern from Java, modern, in front of glass fragments with similar patterns attributed to the 9th-11th century AD.

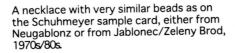

A necklace with very similar beads as on the Schuhmeyer sample card, either from Neugablonz or from Jablonec/Zeleny Brod, 1970s/80s.

Lampworked beads with pulled pattern from Murano/Venice, first third of the twentieth century. The background shows fragments of Roman glass vessels with a similar fancyful mixture of colors and pulled patterns. The pulled pattern dates back to antiquity and had a most splendid revival on the blown glass of the Art Nouveau period.

A sample card including beads with trailings and pulled pattern, Murano/Venice, nineteenth century. (Glass Museum Murano). The pulled pattern had presumably been reactivated in Murano/Venice in the late eighteenth century.

Seven beads with pulled pattern from Murano, 1950s. These beads are additionally covered with tiny glass globules, named "ballotini." They are not glued but molten upon the surface of the bead. This variety of beads is very rare.

A vase with pulled pattern from Germany, 1920s/30s, and a paperweight with an "Art Nouveau" type design from the Okra glass-studio in England, 1986. This pulled pattern was very fashionable during the first third of the twentieth century.

A necklace with pulled pattern beads from Murano/Venice, 1988. The pulled pattern design is still made in many variations.

Four necklaces including beads with pulled pattern, Murano/Venice, 1920s/30s. These necklaces are strung in the original way with small wound spacer beads in a color which matches the colors on the large beads. The color combinations on these pulled-pattern-beads are generally very sophisticated.

A necklace including beads with a trailed decoration  similar to the vase on p. 180, Murano, 1970s. A colored core has been overlaid with crystal glass and additionally entwined with crystal trailings. The old pattern finds always new and imaginative reinterpretations.

A necklace including beads with pulled pattern from Murano/Venice, possibly early twentieth century. These beads are quite exceptional. Each bead includes every possible color - ranging from white to black and including yellow, orange, red, blue, green, brown, and aventurine - and yet the mixture is so very well done that they don't look too colorful.

A vase from the Salviati company in
Venice, circa 1960s.

Black beads with fancy trailings from
Murano/Venice, 20th century. This type of
bead was meant for the African trade. The
black core is entwined with fragments of
complex canes. Two crystal beads with
fancy trailings, of uncertain origin, possibly
Gablonz, 1920s/30s. The beads were
created for the fasionable European
market. They are equally deorated with
complex canes yet those canes have
quite uncommon color combinations - a
white core with brown and black stripes.

# THE FUTURE OF EUROPEAN BEAD ART AND CRAFT

The European bead industries inherited a major part of their bead glass technology, their beadmaking techniques, even their bead patterns from the Middle East from antiquity. They perfected the technologies and procedures through the centuries and they composed imaginative new types of bead glass. They created innumerable variations to the old patterns as well as entirely new design lines. The European bead industries grew because versatile merchants developed an enormous inland market, because they took over the African market from the Far East industries and they opened the New World market - and last but not least because thousands of anonymous craftsmen and women were exploited. For about 400 years European glass beads ruled the world.

In this century the European bead manufacturers started to feel "the winds of change." Standard production lines in mass-produced beads had to be handed back to Asian bead industries and Asian craftsmen became in the field of certain elaborate beads always stronger competitors on the international markets.

The industrial side of beadmaking has become much more difficult - while the situation for high standard European bead craft has changed towards the better, as an ever growing number of people now appreciate that glass beads are small works of art. European glass beads will have a future as long as their artists are able to reinterpret the millennia-old themes with the unequalled imagination they have demonstrated in this century, especially in recent years.

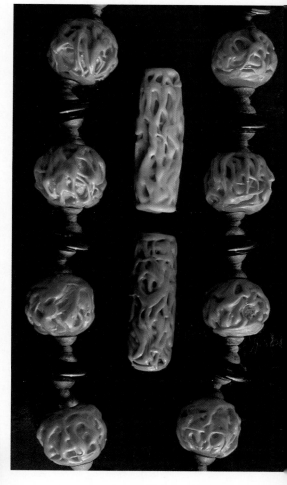

Coral colored and green beads from the Costantini company, Murano, 1992. Such spun beads are a quite rare design line. Similar beads were/are made in Gablonz/Neugablonz.

A brooch with sparkling crystal beads, langani, Stuttgart, circa 1960. This is modern beadwork creativity at its best, achieving imaginative effects with quite standard beads.

A beaded bracelet created by the artist Natacha Wolters, Berlin (Courtesy of N. Wolters). The bracelet is knitted in the artist's own technique in which it is beaded on both sides. The clasp is made with lapis lazuli and silk. The bracelet was created as part of a series on fruits, flowers, and geometry.

langani earpendant "Ninel", 1980s (Courtesy langani, Stuttgart).

langani necklace in 1971. A multistranded artistic interpretation of African necklace design, again achived with quite common beads.

langani brooch "Ersari", circa 1989
(Courtesy langani, Stuttgart).

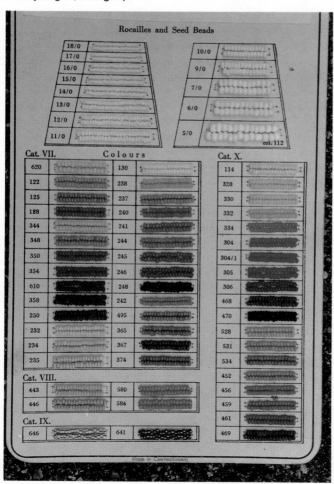

Necklace "Peacock" created by the beadartist Helga Seimel, Landsberg/ Germany (Courtesy of H. Seimel; photograph by Noah Cohen). The "leaves" on this necklace are made from transparent glass overlaid with gold foil. The longest leaf measures 5 centimeters and the total length of the necklace is 46 centimeters. The artist was born in Augsburg and started lampworking in 1974. She opened her own workshop in Landsberg in 1988. Her jewelry is included in the collections of important museums such as the Glass Museum Frauenau, the Bead Museum in Prescott/ Arizona, and the Corning Museum of Glass/ New York.

A sample card with "Rocailles," Jablonec, 1960s. The North Bohemian bead industry creates the finest possible "seed" beads in many delicate shades.

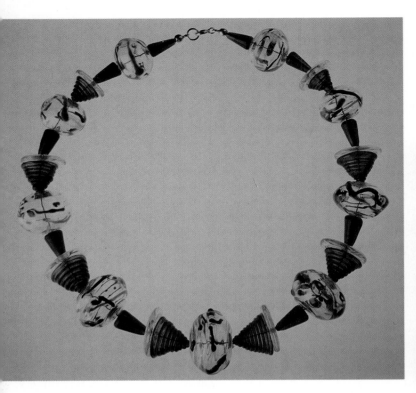

A close-up of the beads from the Glaser necklace. The effect of the necklace is due to the sophisticated combination of seven different shades in blue and green but also to the labor-intensive extra work which has been given to some beads. They are cut and polished on four facets to enhance their satiny sheen.

Necklace with imaginative lampworked beads created by the artist Helga Seimel, Landsberg/Germany (Courtesy of H. Seimel; photograph: Braun). Diameter of the beads: 2.5 cm; Length of the necklace: 44 cm. The round and large conical beads are wrapped hollow beads, crafted in the artist's own technique.

She crafts some of her beads in this very special and difficult technique because it enables her to create a wider variety of imaginative beads, as the choice of colors in massive canes - out of which the beads are wrapped - is much larger than in tubes for blowing beads. The beads thus created can be in addition very large without becoming too heavy. The round crystal beads are further decorated with blue and green trailings.

The structure of the wrapping is visible on the conical beads. Their conus is "closed" with a crystal rondel which is separately strung.

The smaller conical beads are standard wound beads.

Various strands of lampworked beads created by the artist Helga Seimel, Landsberg/Germany. (Courtesy of H. Seimel; photograph by David Hopper). The artist Helga Seimel masters perfectly the classical techniques and patterns and recombines them into entirely new bead design. Her necklaces offer not only eye-catching attractiveness but also intricate craftmanship on each single bead.

A five-stranded necklace from A. F. Glaser,
Neugablonz, circa 1990.
Elaborate beads assembled into an eye-
catching necklace.

Elaborate beads from agate-colored
glass, A. F. Glaser, Neugablonz, 1980s. The
beads were carefully molded and got a
matte finish. Additionally they were cut and
polished on two flat facets to reveal the
delicate internal colors.

A Grossé brooch, 1992 and corresponding
beads from Emil Elstner, Neugablonz, 1991.

Three very elaborate modern eye beads
from Murano. The large bead has 28
"eyes."

A beaded rose of Nella Lopez y Royo Sammartini, Venice, 1993. The century-old craft of beaded flowers had been reactivated by this artist in a most splendid perfection.

An elaborate necklace from Neugablonz, 1970s.

A necklace from Murano/Venice, 1994. This is a most sophisticated version of foil beads. A gold-foiled core is covered with crystal and additionally covered by abundant trailings in orange and yellow transparent glass.

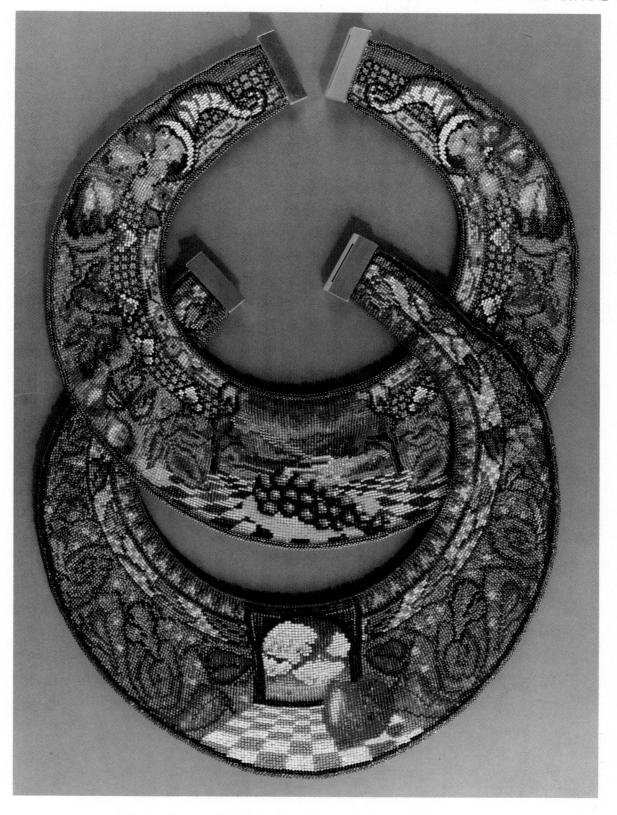

Two beaded necklaces "Summer" and "Autumn" created by the artist Natacha Wolters, Berlin (Courtesy of N. Wolters; photograph by C. Wolters). The artist had been experimenting to find a new knitting technique which gave her the possiblity to work on the form of the object. Each necklace is beaded on both sides and counts almost 40,000 beads.

The center of each necklace shows a miniature landscape. Natacha Wolters has been trained in painting and sees her pieces of jewelry as a continuation of her pictorial art. She considers the combination of beads and textile an interesting surface, offering the sensorial contrasts hard and soft and cold and warm and producing ever changing effects due to the varying interaction between the glass beads and the light. Her beaded wall art is absolutely fascinating and her beaded pictures invite meditation and dream travels.

# BIBLIOGRAPHY

Africanus, Leo. *The History and Description of Africa...*Translated from the Italian by John Pory and edited by R. Brown, London, 1896.

AIHV 1985:

*Annales du 10e congrès de l'Association Internationale pour l'Histoire du Verre.* Madrid-Segovie, 23-28 septembre 1985; Amsterdam, *AIHV*, 1987.

AIHV 1991:*Annales du 12e congrès de l'AIHV.* Vienne, 26-31 août 1991; Amsterdam, *AIHV*, 1993.

AIHV 1988:

*Annales du 11e congrès de l'AIHV.* Bâle, 29 août - 3 septembre 1988; Amsterdam, *AIHV*, 1990.

Alénus-Lecerf, J. "Decouvertes Récentes...," *AIHV* 1985: 221-236.

Baart, J. M. et al. *Herstellung und Gebrauch von Trinkglas in Amsterdam (1580-1640).* Spechtergläser: Ausstellung im Glasmuseum Wertheim, 1986.

Barag, Dan P. "The Prelude to Hellenistic Gold Glass," *AIHV* 1988: 19-26.

Barbosa, Duarte. *The Book of Duarte Barbosa.* London: Hakluyt Society, 1918.

Barovier-Mentasti, Rosa. *Il Vetro Veneziano.* Milano: Electa Spa, 1982.

Barrelet, J. *La Verrerie en France.* Paris, 1953.

Barrera, J. "La Verrerie Médiévale d'Etampes," *AIHV* 1988: 341-346.

Barrera, J. "La verrerie du XIVe au XVIe Siècles...," *AIHV* 1985: 341-360.

Barta, J. *Alte. Glasmachergeschlechter in Böhmen.* Sprechsaal: Coburg, 1936-1943.

Barth, Heinrich. *Reisen und Entdeckungen in Nord- und Centralafrika in den Jahren1849-1855.* Gotha, 1857.

Baumgartner, E. & Krüger, I. *Phönix aus Sand und Asche.* München: Klinkhardt & Biermann, 1988.

Bayley, J. "Viking Glassworking - the evidence from York," *AIHV* 1985: 245-254.

Bernatzik, Hugo A. *GariGari.* Frankfurt: Gutenberg, 1948.

Bimson, M. & Freestone, I. C. "The Discovery of an Islamic Glassmaking Site in Middle Egypt," *AIHV,* 1985: 237-244.

Blake, J. W. *Europeans in West Africa.* London: Hakluyt Society, 1942.

Blau, J. "Patterlmacher und Patterlhütten im Böhmerwald," *Glastechnische Berichte,* 1941: 89-97.

Blau, J. *Die Glasmacher im Böhmer- und Bayernwald...* (reprint). Grafenau: Morsak Verlag, 1983.

Blau, J. *Die Glasmacher...Familienkunde* (reprint). Grafenau: Morsak Verlag, 1984.

Bontemps, G. *Le Guide du Verrier.* Paris, 1868.

Braun/Barth. *Herodot - das Geschichtswerk.* Berlin & Weimar: Aufbau Verlag, 1985.

Brauneck, M. *Religiöse Volkskunst.* Köln: DuMont Verlag, 1978.

Brentjes, B. *Fels- und Höhlenbilder Africas.* Leipzig: Köhler & Amelang, no date.

Brepohl, E. *Theophilus Presbyter.* Wien/Köln/Graz: Böhlau Verlag, 1987.

Bussolin, Domenico, *Guida Alle Fabbriche Vetrarie di Murano.* Venezia, 1842.

Caillaud, Frédéric. *Voyage à Meroe...1819-1822.* Paris, no date.

Caillié, René. *Journal d'un Voyage à Temboctou et à Jenné...* Paris: Imprimerie Royale, 1830.

Carey, M. *Beads and Beadwork of East and South Africa.* London: Shire Publications, 1986.

Cecchetti, B. & Zanetti, V. *Monografia Della Vetreria Veneziana e Muranese.* Venezia: Antonelli, 1874.

Cecchetti, B. *La Vita dei Veneziani nel 1300.* Venezia: Tipografia Emiliana, 1886.

Claude, D. *Der Handel im Westlichen Mittelmeer Während des Frühmittelalters.* Göttingen, Vandenhoeck & Ruprecht, 1985.

Cristalleri, Mariegola, Venezia: Archivio di Stato, mariegola 99

Cucchetti, F. *Tre Documenti del Secolo Scorso (1754).* Venezia, 1884.

Cunnison, Ian. *King Kazembe...* Lisbon, 1960.

Cuvelier, J. *L'ancien Royaume de Congo.* Bruxelles, 1946.

Dannheimer, H. & Gebhard, R. *Das Keltische Jahrtausend.* Mainz: Philipp von Zabern, 1993.

Davidson, Basil. *Africa in History.* London: Orion Books, 1992.

Defrémery, C. & Sanguinetti, B. R. *Ibn Batoutah.* Paris, 1863.

Dekowna, M. "Les Perles en Verre...," *AIHV,* 1991: 271-278.

*Deutsches Kolonialblatt.* Berlin: 1890 - 1900.

Diderot & D'Alembert. *Encyclopédie Méthodique...* Paris: 1751-1777.

Diop, Cheik Anta. *The African Origin of Civilization.* Chicago: Lawrence Hill Books, 1974.

Düwel, K. et al. *Untersuchungen zu Handel und Verkehr...* Göttingen: Vandenhoeck & Ruprecht, 1985.

Eyo, Ekpo & Willett, Frank. *Kunstschätze aus Alt-Nigeria.* Mainz: Philipp von Zabern, 1983.

Fischer, Karl R. *Die Schürer von Waldheim.* Prag: Verlag des Vereins für Geschichte der Deutschen in Böhmen, 1924.

Friedl, P. *Glasmachergeschichten und Glashüttensagen...* Grafenau: Morsak Verlag, 1973.

Gasparetto, A. *Il Vetro di Murano.* Venezia: Neri Pozza Editore, 1958.

Gerspach. *L'art de La Verrerie.* Paris: A. Quantin, 1885.

Gozzi, G. *Intorno ai Mezzi di far Rifiorire...(1761), Scrittura edita di V. Zanetti.* Venezia, 1869.

Grimm, C. *Glück und Glas - Zur Kulturgeschichte des Spessartglases.* München: Verlag Kunst & Antiquitäten, 1984.

Hachmann, R. *Frühe Phöniker im Libanon.* Mainz: Philipp von Zabern, 1983.

Haevernik, Thea E. *Beiträge zur Glasforschung.* Mainz: Philipp von Zabern, 1981.

Hakluyt, Richard, *The Principal Navigations...* 8 volumes, London: J. M. Dent & Co., New York: E. P. Dutton & Co., no date.

Hall, Martin. *The Changing Past...* Cape Town & Johannesburg: David Philip Publishers, 1987.

Haller, R. *Geschundenes Glas.* Grafenau: Morsak Verlag, 1985.

Haller, R. *Historische Glashütten.* Grafenau: Morsak Verlag, 1981.

Hansenmann, L. *Amulett und Talisman.* München: Callwey Verlag, 1966.

Henderson, Julian. "Bronze Age Glass in Europe," *AIHV,* 1988: 1-10.

Henderson, Julian, "Aspects of Early Medieval Glassproduction in Britain," *AIHV,* 1991: 247-260.

Henderson, Julian. "Chemical and Archeological Analysis of Some British and European Prehistoric Glasses," *AIHV,* 1985: 13-22.

Henkes, Harold E. *Glas Zonder Glans.* Rotterdam, 1994.

Herbst, H. *Der Bericht des Franziskaners Wilhelm von Rumburk über seine Reise 1253-1255...*Leipzig, 1925.

Herm, G. *Die Phönizier.* Reinbek/Hamburg: Rowohlt Verlag, 1987.

Hibbert, Christopher. *Africa Explored.* London: Penguin Books, 1982.

Hoffmann, R. *Lauschaer Glaskunst Heute.* Lauscha, 1972.

Hoffmann, R. *Zur Sozialen Lage der Werktätigen in der Lauschaer Glasindustrie.* Lauscha, no date.

Hoffmann, R. *Thüringer Glaskunst Gestern und Heute.* Lauscha, 1978.

Hoffmann, Rudi. *Das Museum für Glaskunst Lauscha.* Lauscha, 1971.

Hornung, E. *Gesänge vom Nil.* Zürich & München: Artemis Verlag, 1990.

Ilg, A. *Studien auf dem Gebiet des Kunstgewerblichen Unterrichts in Italien.* Wien, 1875.

*Industrie des Thüringer Waldes.* Deutsche Gewerbezeitung, 1858: 126-132.

Jannin, F. "Les Verreries Médiévales d'Argonnes," *AIHV,* 1988: 317-324.

Jargstorf, S. *Baubles, Buttons and Beads.* Atglen: Schiffer Publishing, 1993.

Jones, Steve, *The Language of the Genes;* London, HarperCollins, 1993.

Junkers, W. *Reisen in Afrika 1875-1886.* Wien & Olmütz, 1889.

Kalashnikova, N. & Pluzhnikova, G. *National costumes of the Soviet People.* Moscow: Planeta Publishers, 1990.

Kisa. *Das Glas im Altertume.* Leipzig, 1908.

Köhler, K. *Die Entwicklung der Tracht.* Nürnberg: F. Herdegen, 1877.

Krüger, I. "Glassmirrors in Medieval times," *AIHV,* 1991: 319-332.

Kühnert, H. *Urkundenbuch zur Thüringischen Glashüttengeschichte.* Wiesbaden: Franz Steiner, 1973.

Kunckel, Johannes. *Ars Vitraria oder Glasmacherkunst.* Frankfurt and Leipzig: Chr. Riegel, 1689.

Lardner, Dionysius. *The Cabinet Cyclopedia.* London: Longman, Rees, Orme, Brown, and Green, 1832.

*Le Vaillants erste Reise in das Innere von Afrika während der Jahre 1780-1782.* Berlin: Christian F. Voss, 1790.

Lindskog-Wallenberg, G. *Frauenkleidungsstücke und Kleiderschmuck im Mittelniederdeutschen.* Berlin, 1977.

Littmann, E. "Äthiopische Inschriften," *Miscellanea Academica Berolinensia* II/2 1950: 97-110.

Löber, Ernst. *Zur Geschichte der Lampenglasblaserei auf dem Thüringer Wald.* Weimar: Glas & Apparat, 1926.

Lopez y Royo Sammartini, N. *Fiori di perle a Venezia.* Venezia: Centro Internazionale Della Grafica di Venezia, 1992.

Loth, Heinrich. *Die Frau im Alten Afrika.* Leipzig: Edition Leipzig, 1986.

Ludolff, Hiob. *Schaubühne der Welt.* Frankfurt, 1716.

Lund-Hansen, U. "Neues aus der Glasforschung in Skandinavien," *AIHV,* 1991: 235-246.

Mares. *Ceske Sklo.* Prag, 1893.

Margariteri, mariegola; Venezia: Archivio di Stato, mariegola 33.

Martell, P. *Zur Geschichte der Glasindustrie und Töpferei in Thüringen.* Die Glashütte, 30/1934: 495-496.

Massa, A. *Les Etrusques.* Genève: Minerva, 1973.

Mecklenburg, A. F. Herzog zu. *Vom Kongo zum Niger und Nil.* Leipzig: Brockhaus, 1912.

Mendera, M. "Some Aspects of Medieval Glassproduction in Central Italy; *AIHV,* 1988: 303-316.

Miani, M. et al. *L'arte dei Maestri vetrai di Murano.* Treviso: Matteo Editore, 1984.

Minutoli, Heinrich C. von. *Nachträge...* Berlin: Maurersche Buchhandlung, 1827.

Minutoli, Heinrich C. von. *Über die Anfertigung und die Nutzanwendung der farbigen Gläser bei den Alten.* Berlin: Maurersche Buchhandlung, 1836.

Minutoli, Heinrich C. von. *Reise zum Tempel des Juppiter Ammon.* Berlin: August Rücker, 1824.

Moiseenko, E. & Faleeva V. *Beadwork in Russia.* Leningrad: Khudoznik, 1990.

Monticolo, G. & Besta, E. *I capitolari Delle Arti Veneziane Dalle Origine al 1330.* Roma, 1914.

Morazzoni, G. & Pasquato, M. *Le conterie Veneziane.* Venezia: Società Veneziana Conterie e Cristallerie, 1953.

*Münzen in Brauch und Aberglauben.* Mainz: Philipp von Zabern, 1982.

Nachtigal, G. *Sahara und Sudan.* Berlin: 1879.

Neri, Antonio. *L'arte Vetraria 1612* (commented reprint). Milano: Edizioni il polifilo, 1980.

Neuwirth, Waltraud. *Beads from Gablonz, Historicism, Art Nouveau.* Wien, Selbstuerlag Dr. W. Neuwirth, 1994.

Newby, M. "Medieval Glass from Farfa," *AIHV,* 1985: 255-270.

Ninni, Irene. *L'impiraressa.* Venezia, 1893.

Paiva-Manso, Visconde de. *Historia do Congo.* Lisboa, 1877.

Pazaurek, Gustav E. "Altthüringischer Glasschnitt," *Glastechnische Berichte* 9/1933: 325-330.

Péligot, E. *Le Verre.* Paris: G. Masson, 1877.

*Perle e Impiraperle.* Venezia: Arsenale Editrice, 1990.

Petermann, A. & Hassenstein, B. *Inner-Afrika...im Jahre 1861.* Gotha: Justus Perthes, 1862.

Phillipson, David W. *African Archeology.* Cambridge: University Press, 1993.

Pinkerton. *A General Collection of the Best and Most Interesting Voyages and Travels...* London, 1814.

Pischel, Barbara. *Die Thüringische Glasblaserei.* Weimar, 1936.

Pischel, Felix. *Thüringische Glashüttengeschichte.* Weimar, 1928.

Pittrof, Kurt. *Böhmisches Glas im Panorama der Jahrhunderte.* München: R. Oldenbourg Verlag, 1989.

Pliny. Naturalis Historiae.

Polo, Marco. *Milione* (commented reprint). Milano: Adelphi Edizione, 1975.

Poschinger-Buchenau, K. von. *Die Entstehung der Glashütten in der Umgebung von Zwiesel und Grafenau.* Monatsschrift f.d. bayr. Grenzmarken, 1921: 53-55.

Praxl, Paul. "Die Ältesten Glashütten des Böhmerwaldes," *Passauer Jahrbuch* 1983: 71-79.

Puschkarjow, W. *Russische Angewandte Kunst.* Leningrad: Aurora Publishers, 1976.

Ravenstein, E. G. (ed). *A Journal of the First Voyage of Vasco da Gama.* London, Hakluyt Society, 1898.

Ritsema van Eck, P. C. "Sources for Glassengraving in the Netherlands in the 17th Century," *AIHV,* 1985: 437-448.

Ritz, G. *Die Christlichegebetszählschnur.* München, 1955.

Rohlf, Gerhard. *Reise Durch Nordafrika 1865-67.* Gotha: Justus Perthes, 1868.

Saint-Martin, V. de. *Le Nord de L'afrique dans L'antiquité Grecque et Romaine.* Paris: Imprimerie Royale, 1863.

Saleh, M. & Sourouzian, H. *Das Ägyptische Museum Kairo.* Mainz: Philipp von Zabern, 1986.

Schachtzabel, Alfred. *Im Hochland von Angola.* Dresden: Deutsche Werkstätten, 1923.

Schaedel, E. *Ein Leben für das Glas.* Kranichfeld: Hahndruck, 1990.

Schapera, I. & Farrington, B. (ed). *The Early Cape Hottentots.* Cape Town: Van Riebeck Society, 1933.

Schebek, Edmund. *Böhmens Glasindustrie und Glashandel* (reprint). Frankfurt/M, 1969.

Schreiber, E. *Die Glasblasekunst....* Weimar: B. F. Voigt, 1849.

Schweidt, H. "Thüringer Industrie," *Friedrich Georg Wieck's Deutsche Illustrierte Gewerbezeitung,* 17/1864: 129-132; 24/1864: 185-188; 26/1864: 201-204; 29/1864: 225-227.

Schweinfurth, Georg. *Im Herzen von Afrika...1868-1871.* Leipzig, Bockhaus, 1922.

Sellner, Chr. *Der Gläserne Wald.* München: Prestel Verlag, 1988.

Seyfert, I. "Die Poschinger von Frauenau," *Beiträge zur Heimatkunde von Niederbayern,* III, *Landshut* 1976: 201-222.

Stahl, C. J. *Die Glasdrückerei.* Dresden: Verlag Die Glashütte, 1926.

*Stanley in Africa.* London: Walter Scott Ltd., no date.

Stanley, H. M. *Der Kongo.* Leipzig: Brockhaus, 1885.

Stenger, A. *Verreries and Verriers au pays de Sarrebourg.* Sarrebourg: SHAL, 1988.

Stephan, H-G. "Mittelalterliche Glasproduktion...," *AIHV,* 1988: 291-302.Stern, E. M. "Early Roman Glass from Heis on the North Somali Coast," *AIHV,* 1985: 23-36.

Stern, M. & Schlick-Nolte, B. *Frühes Glas der alten Welt.* Stuttgart, Gerd Hatje Verlag, 1994.

Stout, Ann M. "An Investigation of Mosaic Glass Face Beads," *AIHV,* 1991: 99-110.

Theobald, W. *Technik des Kunsthandwerks im 12. Jahrhundert* Düsseldorf: VDI-Verlag, 1984.

Venclova, N. "Late Bronze and Early Iron Age Glass in Czechoslovakia," *AIHV,* 1988, pages 11-17.

*Verhandlungen des Historischen Vereins für Niederbayern,* Landshut, 1890.

*Verhandlungen des Historischen Vereins für Niederbayern,* Landshut, 1856.

Voronov, N. & Rachuk, E. *Soviet Glass.* Leningrad: Aurora Publishers, 1973.

Wagner, H. *Die neuesten Entdeckungsreisen an der Westküste Afrika's.* Leipzig: Otto Spamer, 1863.

Wagner, H. "Die Anfänge der Glashütten um Grafenau," *Passauer Jahrbuch* 1960: 107-113.

Wallace-Dunlop, M. A. *Glass in the Old World.* London: Field & Tuer, Leadenhall Presse; Simpkin, Marshall & Co.; Hamilton, Adams & Co. New York: Scribner & Welford, 743 & 745 Broadway, no date, late 19th century.

Webster, L. & Backhouse, J. *The Making of England...* London: British Museum Press, 1991.

Wikinger, Waräger, Normannen. *Mainz.* Philipp von Zabern, 1992.

Zanetti, V. *Esposizione Vetraria Muranese nel 1864.* Venezia, 1864.

Zanetti, V. *Guida di Murano.* Venezia, 1866.

Zanetti, V. *Cenni Biografici di Giovanni Giacomuzzi.* Venezia: Longo, 1872.

Zanetti, V. *La perla di vetro color giallo d'oro...* Venezia, 1870.

Zanetti, V. *Lavori alla lucerna.* Venezia: P. Naratovich, 1867.

Zecchin, Luigi. *Il ricettario Darduin.* Venezia: Arsenale editrice, 1986.

Zecchin, Luigi. *Vetro e vetrai di Murano, volume I - III.* Venezia: Arsenale editrice, 1987, 1989, 1990.

Zenkner, Karl. *Die alten Glashütten im Isergebirge;* Schwäbisch-Gmünd: Leutelt Gesellschaft, 1968.

Zucchello, Pignol. *Lettere di mercanti a P. Z. (1336-1350).* Venezia: Il comitato editore, 1957.

# VALUE GUIDE

| Page & Position | Description | Value (£ Sterling) |
|---|---|---|
| 5 TR | Rudraksha bead necklace | 15-25 |
| 5 BR | German necklace | 10-12 |
| | Indian necklace | 10-15 |
| 8 TL | String Turkish beads | 5-10 |
| 11 TR | Strand Bavarian beads | 10-15 |
| | Strand Indian beads | 2-5 |
| 10 TR | Lampworked bead | 3-5 |
| 10 BL | Strand Indonesian beads | 15-20 |
| 13 TR | C. Balbi head bead | 20-30 |
| 13 BL | Bohemian bangle | 5-10 |
| | Strand Bavarian beads | 10-15 |
| 13 BR | String Ringlet beads | 35-45 |
| 14 T | Necklace Indian beads | 25-35 |
| 15 BR | Roman mosaic beads | RARE |
| 15 BL | Lampworked bead | 3-4 |
| 16 TR | Roman bead | RARE |
| | WMF necklace | 200-300 |
| 16 TL | Necklace Murano | 15-20 |
| | Indian millefiori bead | 1 |
| 20 TL | Trade bead | 1.50-3 |
| 23 TR | Strand Turkish coiled beads | 2-3 |
| | Large Turkish bead | 1 |
| 28 BR | Bohemian necklace | 20-30 |
| 41 TL | Nagaland necklace | 50-150 |
| 41 BL | Nagaland necklace | 50-150 |
| 41 TR | Indian necklace | 10-20 |
| 41 BR | Strand Indonesian beads | 15-20 |
| 44 TR | langani necklace | 40-90 |
| | langani brooch | 25-30 |
| 45 TR | "Pearl" strands | RARE |
| 45 B | Strand "stone" beads | 5-10 |
| 47 BR | Rosetta beads | RARE |
| 49 B | Moretti bead | 1.50-3 |
| | Strand lampworked beads | 25-40 |
| 53 BR | Strand drawn beads | 15-25 |
| 54 TR | Aventurine bead | 3-4 |
| 55 TL | Indian necklace | 20-40 |
| 55 TR | Beadwork necklace | 20-25 |
| 59 BR | Moretti bead | 3-4 |
| 59 TL | Blown bead | 5-8 |
| 59 TR | Strand "coral" beads | RARE |
| 62 TR | African necklace | 5-10 |
| | Lampworked bead | 4-8 |
| 65 TL | Lampworked bead | 3-4 |
| 65 TR | Gold pendant | 20-40 |
| 65 BR | Trade bead | 1.50-3 |
| 66 TL | Moretti necklace | RARE |
| 67 TL | Moretti necklaces | 15-50 |
| 67 B | Moretti necklace | 30 |
| 68 BR | Blown bead | 3-5 |
| 69 CR | Costantini bead | 5 |
| 71 TR | Nagaland necklace | 90-170 |
| 71 BR | Strand blue beads | 90-120 |
| 72 TL | Trade bead | 3-4 |
| | Strand red beads | 40-80 |
| | Red bead | 2-3 |
| 73 TR | Opalescent bead | RARE |
| 73 BR | Strand opalescent beads | 40-80 |
| 74 TL | Birnel strand | 90-145 |
| 75 BR | Strand of gold-lined bugles | RARE |
| 76 BR | Crown | 120-150 |
| | Flower | 6-12 |
| 76 BL | Rousselet necklace | 20-30 |
| 77 TL | Necklace | 20-40 |
| 78 TL | Rousselet necklace | 20-30 |
| 80 TR | Bag | 10-15 |
| 81 TL | Set | 5 |
| 81 TR | Strand "Russian" beads | 20-40 |
| 82 TL | Russian necklace | 5-10 |
| 82 BL | Candle holder | 20-40 |
| 84 TL | Christmas decoration | 3-5 |
| 85 TR | Strands of blown beads | RARE |
| 85 BR | Bead/marble | 10-35 |
| 87 TL | Necklace | 10-20 |
| 87 TR | Schaedel necklace | 90-150 |
| 88 TR | Strand "Taubeneiperlen" | 95-135 |
| 88 BR | Basket | 5-15 |
| 89 CR | Mats | 5-7 |
| | Holders | 7-10 |
| 89 CL | Strand Bavarian beads | 10-15 |
| 89 BL | langani necklace | 40-90 |
| 90 BL | Bobbin | 7-10 |
| 91 TL | Strand faceted beads | 95-150 |
| 92 BR | Strand blown beads | 5-10 |
| 93 BR | Bead | 2-4 |
| 94 CR | Buckle | 8-12 |
| 94 BR | Christmas decoration | 8-15 |
| 95 TL | Necklaces | 15-20 |
| 95 CR | Necklaces | 15-25 |
| 95 BL | Christmas decoration | 8-15 |
| 96 TL | Necklace | 15-25 |
| 96 BR | Christmas decoration | 8-15 |
| 96 TR | Strand | 10-25 |
| 98 TR | Necklace | 20-40 |
| 99 BR | Necklaces | 20-40 |
| 100 TR | Necklace | 20-30 |
| 100 BR | Necklace | 20-35 |
| 101 TL | Necklace | 15-25 |
| 101 B | Necklaces | 15-30 |
| 101 TR | Necklace | 20-30 |
| 102 TL | Necklace | 15-20 |
| 102 TR | Table Mat | 3-7 |
| 103 TR | Necklaces | 5-7 |
| 103 B | Necklace | 15-30 |
| 104 TL | Earpendants | 22 |
| 104 BL | Necklaces | 8-12 |
| 104 TR | Strand | 5-10 |
| 104 TC | Strand | 5-10 |
| 107 B | Rosetta beads | RARE |
| 109 TR | "Nueva Cadiz" bead | RARE (N.Y. $16-20) |
| 109 BL | Strand | 90-135 |
| 111 B | Maurentanian bead | RARE |
| 112 TR | Strand "Birnel" | 90-145 |
| 112 BR | Trade bead | 2-4 |
| 114 TL | Costume doll | 7-10 |
| 114 TR | African necklace | 10-12 |
| 114 BR | Yoruba belt | 70-110 |
| 114 BL | Yoruba belt | 70-110 |
| 121 TR | Norweigan belt | 15-20 |
| 121 B | English beadwork | 20-25 |
| 122 B | African beadwork | 10-18 |
| 123 BR | African belt | 15-20 |
| 123 CR | African beadwork | 5-8 |
| 125 TR | Opalescent bead | 4-7 |
| 125 BL | "Pearl" necklaces | 20-30 |